Baumann

Editor
Cassandra K. Burton, M. Ed.

Editorial Project Manager
Ina Massler Levin, M.A.

Editor-in-Chief
Sharon Coan, M.S. Ed.

Illustrator
Victoria Panikvar Frazier

Cover Artist
Charles Adler

Art Coordinator
Denice Adorno

Creative Director
Elayne Roberts

Imaging
Alfred Lau
Rosa C. See

Product Manager
Phil Garcia

Publishers
Rachelle Cracchiolo, M.S. Ed.
Mary Dupuy Smith, M.S. Ed.

Descriptive Writing
Grades 1–2

Written by
Jennifer Overend Prior, M. Ed. and Diana Stephens

Teacher Created Materials, Inc.
6421 Industry Way
Westminster, CA 92683
www.teachercreated.com

ISBN-1-57690-986-7

©2000 Teacher Created Materials, Inc.
Made in U.S.A.

Table of Contents

Introduction

Teaching descriptive writing is an exciting process for students. It allows them to learn ways to express themselves and share with others creatively.

The Descriptive Writing Unit

The lessons in this book will help your students write descriptive stories, poems, and paragraphs through the use of adjectives, adverbs, details, and figurative language. They will learn to develop the content of their writing through lessons about narrowing topics and using graphic organizers.

Through descriptive writing, your students will also be able to perfect basic writing skills. This book contains a section of activities for using correct punctuation, capitalization, complete sentences, nouns, proper nouns, verbs, adjectives, and adverbs.

Each lesson provides a teacher-directed activity followed by one or more worksheets for student practice. Some of the lessons even provide learning center games for additional exposure to the skills. Because the lessons are complete within themselves, they can be taught in any order.

The skills within each lesson are grade-level appropriate and linked to the Writing Standards. On pages 4–6, you'll find a list of the standards for kindergarten through second grade. At the top of each lesson, a reference to one or more of these standards is indicated. By using every lesson in this book, you can be sure that your students will be exposed to all of the skills needed in order to move toward mastery of the Language Arts Standards.

By integrating these lessons into your language arts program, your students will strengthen their basic writing skills while creating written work that can be shared with others. Feel free to allow your students' creativity to flow. They will enjoy adding illustrations and computer graphics to their work, create their own borders for written work, and certainly display and share their completed work.

The Assessment Section

The assessment section of this book provides a variety of tools for evaluating student work. Included are several rubrics appropriate for different types of writing assessment. You'll also find a self-assessment sheet for the students and a skills checklist for you to record mastery of the standards.

Standards for Language Arts
Grades K-2

Accompanying the major activities of this book will be references to the basic standards and benchmarks for writing that will be met by successful performance of the activities. Each specific standard and benchmark will be referred to by the appropriate letter and number from the following collection. For example, a basic standard and benchmark identified as **1A** would be as follows:

Standard 1: Demonstrates competence in the general skills and strategies of the writing process

Benchmark A: Prewriting: Uses prewriting strategies to plan written work (e.g., discusses ideas with peers, draws pictures to generate ideas, writes key thoughts and questions, rehearses ideas, records reactions and observations)

A standard and benchmark identified as **4B** would be as follows:

Standard 4: Gathers and uses information for research purposes

Benchmark B: Uses books to gather information for research topics (e.g., uses table of contents, examines pictures and charts)

Clearly, some activities will address more than one standard. Moreover, since there is a rich supply of activities included in this book, some will overlap in the skills they address, and some, of course, will not address every single benchmark within a given standard. Therefore, when you see these standards referenced in the activities, refer to this section for complete descriptions.

Although virtually every state has published its own standards and every subject area maintains its own lists, there is surprising commonality among these various sources. For the purposes of this book, we have elected to use the collection of standards synthesized by John S. Kendall and Robert J. Marzano in their book *Content Knowledge: A Compendium of Standards and Benchmarks for K-12 Education* (second edition 1997) as illustrative of what students at various grade levels should know and be able to do. The book is published jointly by McREL (Mid-continent Regional Educational Laboratory, Inc.) and ASCD (Association for Supervision and Curriculum Development). (Used by permission of McREL.)

Language Arts Standards

1. Demonstrates competence in the general skills and strategies of the writing process

2. Demonstrates competence in the stylistic and rhetorical aspects of writing

3. Uses grammatical and mechanical conventions in written compositions

4. Gathers and uses information for research purposes

Standards for Language Arts
Grades K–2 *(cont.)*

---

1. Demonstrates competence in the general skills and strategies of the writing process

A. Prewriting: Uses prewriting strategies to plan written work (e.g., discusses ideas with peers, draws pictures to generate ideas, writes key thoughts and questions, rehearses ideas, records reactions and observations)

B. Drafting and Revising: Uses strategies to draft and revise written work (e.g., rereads; rearranges words, sentences, and paragraphs to improve or clarify meaning; varies sentence type; adds descriptive words and details; deletes extraneous information; incorporates suggestions from peers and teachers; sharpens the focus)

C. Editing and Publishing: Uses strategies to edit and publish written work (e.g., proofreads using a dictionary and other resources; edits for grammar, punctuation, capitalization, and spelling at a developmentally appropriate level; incorporates illustrations or photos; shares finished product)

D. Evaluates own and others' writing (e.g., asks questions and makes comments about writing, helps classmates apply grammatical and mechanical conventions)

E. Dictates or writes with a logical sequence of events (e.g., includes a beginning, middle, and ending)

F. Dictates or writes detailed descriptions of familiar persons, places, objects, or experiences

G. Writes in response to literature

H. Writes in a variety of formats (e.g., picture books, letters, stories, poems, information pieces)

---

2. Demonstrates competence in the stylistic and rhetorical aspects of writing.

A. Uses general, frequently used words to convey basic ideas

Standards for Language Arts
Grades K-2 *(cont.)*

3. Uses grammatical and mechanical conventions in written compositions

    A. Forms letters in print and spaces words and sentences

    B. Uses complete sentences in written compositions

    C. Uses declarative and interrogative sentences in written compositions

    D. Uses nouns in written compositions (e.g., nouns for simple objects, family members, community workers, and categories)

    E. Uses verbs in written compositions (e.g., verbs for a variety of situations, action words).

    F. Uses adjectives in written compositions (e.g., uses descriptive words)

    G. Uses adverbs in written compositions (e.g., uses words that answer *how*, *when*, *where*, and *why* questions)

    H. Uses conventions of spelling in written compositions (e.g., spells high frequency, commonly misspelled words from appropriate grade-level list; uses a dictionary and other resources to spell words; spells own first and last name)

    I. Uses conventions of capitalization in written compositions (e.g., first and last names, first word of a sentence)

    J. Uses conventions of punctuation in written compositions (uses periods after declarative sentences, uses question marks after interrogative sentences, uses commas in a series)

4. Gathers and uses information for research purposes

    A. Generates questions about topics of personal interest

    B. Uses books to gather information for research topics (e.g., uses table of contents, examines pictures and charts)

Standards and Benchmarks: 1H, 3A, 3B, 3D, 3H

Recognizing Nouns

It is important for primary students to recognize nouns to give a common vocabulary for use in teaching sentence writing, capitalization of proper nouns, and making plurals.

Goal: Students will identify nouns.

Objectives

1. The student will draw and label pictures of nouns.

2. The student will use nouns in writing.

3. The student will differentiate nouns from words that are not nouns.

Materials

- pictures from magazines or discarded calendars
- copy of a children's word book, such as:

  The Sesame Street Word Book by Tom Leigh or *Little Monster's Word Book* by Mercer Mayer (See the bibliography on page 141.)

- butcher paper
- tempera paint (assorted colors)
- paint brushes
- black marker
- copies of lesson worksheets (pages 10 and 11) for each student

Introduction

1. Begin the lesson by explaining to the students that *nouns* are words that name people, places, or things.

2. Have students look around the room and name as many things as they can see. Reiterate each time that the word is called a noun.

3. Discuss with students some places that they can go, such as, home, school, the park, the playground, the store, church, and the movies, explaining that words that name places are also nouns.

4. Ask the students to name different kinds of people, such as, boys, girls, men, women, moms, dads, aunts, uncles, cousins, teachers, doctors, and clerks. Explain that these words are also nouns.

5. Show calendar or magazine pictures to your students and have them name the nouns pictured.

Recognizing Nouns *(cont.)*

Group Activity

1. Read a children's word book (see Materials list, page 7) to your students. Show and discuss the pictures, especially pages featuring people, places, and things.

2. Divide the class into groups of three or four. Provide butcher paper and tempera paints and have each group paint a mural of a place that is familiar to all of them (e.g., the classroom or school, a nearby park, or a local store or restaurant). Emphasize that they depict as many things that are in that place as they can think of.

3. When the painting is finished, have the groups explain what they have painted and label all of the people, places, and things with a black marker.

4. Display the murals on a wall in the classroom or hallway.

Extension Activity

1. To prepare in advance for this activity, copy the following song frame onto chart paper:

   _____ had a _____.
       (person)   *(place)*

   E-I-E-I-O.

   And on/in that _____ he/she had a _____.
                 (place)   *(thing)*

   E-I-E-I-O.

   With a _____ here and a _____ there,
           (thing)   *(thing)*

   Here a _____, there a _____,
           (thing)   *(thing)*

   Everywhere a _____.
              (thing)

   _____ had a _____.
       (person)   *(thing)*

   E-I-E-I-O.

2. Begin the activity by singing "Old MacDonald had a Farm" with the students. Point out that Old MacDonald is a person, his farm is a place, and his animals are things. This is really a song about nouns.

3. Using the song frame, brainstorm with students names of people, places, and things to fill in the blanks.

Recognizing Nouns *(cont.)*

Extension Activity *(cont.)*

4. Sing the new version of "Old MacDonald." For example:

   Mrs. Johnson (principal) had a **school**.

   E-I-E-I-O.

   And in that **school** she had a **class**.

   E-I-E-I-O.

   With a **paper** here, and a **pencil** there,

   Here a **book**, there a **flag**,

   Everywhere a **lunch bag**.

   Mrs. Johnson had a **school**.

   E-I-E-I-O.

Reinforcing the Skill

1. Give each student a copy of worksheet #1 (page 10), and instruct them to complete each blank with a noun.

2. For more practice with nouns, ask the students to differentiate nouns from words that are not nouns on worksheet #2 (page 11).

3. Written Application: Have each student write a short story about a birthday party. Encourage students to tell where the party took place, who was there, what they had to eat, and what presents were received. When the writing is complete, instruct each student to underline the nouns in his or her story.

Publishing Project

Display the stories on a bulletin board entitled "Nouns at our Birthday Parties."

Computer Connection

Using a word processing program, create a document containing two different sections. Entitle one section "Nouns at School," and the other section "Nouns at Home." Instruct students to type appropriate nouns of their choice in each section.

Evaluation

1. Lesson Objectives: Measure each student's progress by reviewing participation in the classroom mural and performance on the lesson worksheets.

2. Written Application: Use a selected rubric from pages 135–137 to evaluate progress. Record mastery on the skills checklist on pages 138 and 139. If desired, have each student use the self-assessment sheet on page 140 to evaluate his or her work.

Recognizing Nouns
Worksheet #1

Write a noun on each line.

1. I like to eat _____.

2. My _____ loves me a lot.

3. I like to play with my _____.

4. When I go to _____, I have fun.

5. The _____ helps me when I am sick.

6. In school, I listen to my _____.

7. We write with _____.

8. My brother can bounce a _____.

9. When I have a question, I raise my _____.

10. My friend painted a pretty _____.

11. He wants a drink of _____.

12. We often visit our _____.

Recognizing Nouns

Worksheet #2

Circle each noun with a red crayon.

boy	friend	monkey	dress
fast	said	apple	hair
run	water	big	down
ball	paper	book	pull
bat	walk	away	out
happy	cry	tree	desk
dog	flower	funny	door
school	pizza	boat	dish

Draw a picture of a person, a place, and a thing.

Standards and Benchmarks: 1H, 3E

Action Verbs

Recognizing action verbs is necessary for primary students in building complete sentences and beginning work with tenses.

Goal: Students will recognize action verbs in writing.

Objectives

1. The student will act out action verbs.
2. The student will identify action verbs in classroom discussion.
3. The student will identify action verbs in original writing.

Materials

- chart paper
- markers
- copy of *The Sesame Street Word Book* by Tom Leigh
- copy of *No, David or David Goes to School* by David Shannon (See the bibliography on page 141.)
- copies of lesson worksheets (pages 15 and 16) for each student
- per student: stamped envelope from home, addressed to a friend or relative

Introduction

1. Prepare in advance by copying the following song onto chart paper:

> *Read, read, read good books.*
> *Reading's really great.*
> *Books can be your friends you know.*
> *They make great playmates.*
>
> *Laugh, laugh, laugh a lot.*
> *Laughter's good for you*
> *When you laugh I think you'll find*
> *You can't be sad or blue.*
>
> *Tell, tell, tell the truth.*
> *Never tell a lie.*
> *When you tell the truth you'll feel*
> *Better by and by.*

Action Verbs *(cont.)*

Introduction *(cont.)*

2. Copy this last verse onto a separate sheet of chart paper:

> *Verbs, verbs, verbs are words*
> *that show activity.*
> *Words like make, and cut, and go,*
> *whisper, ring, and see.*

3. To introduce action verbs, sing "Row, Row, Row Your Boat" with your students. Have them sit on the floor while singing and doing rowing motions.

4. Explain that we call words that talk about something we do, action verbs. Ask the students which words in "Row, Row, Row Your Boat" are *action verbs*.

5. Explain that we could create more verses to "Row, Row, Row Your Boat" by changing the words in the song.

6. Using the prepared song on chart paper, sing the new verses with the students, emphasizing each time that the first three words of each verse are action verbs. Have the students use hand or body motions for the words as they sing.

7. Display the final verse to sing with students as a way to remember the definition for verbs.

Group Activity

1. From *The Sesame Street Word Book*, read pages 20 and 21, "Helping Around the House," to the students. Discuss the pictures and point out the verbs. (Or any other book that features a variety of verbs.)

2. Ask for volunteers to act out things they do to help around the house. Have the other students guess what is being portrayed.

3. Read *No, David* or *David Goes to School,* and discuss the pictures. As students suggest action verbs portrayed in the pictures, write their responses on chart paper and post in the classroom.

Extension Activity

1. Cross-curricular Connection: When discussing community helpers in social studies, list the things people do every day on chart paper. In science, discuss and list action verbs when talking about animals, pets, dinosaurs, insects, volcanoes, rivers, weather, or storms.

Action Verbs *(cont.)*

Extension Activity *(cont.)*

2. Record a list of action verbs supplied by the students in a classroom discussion of their daily routines.

Reinforcing the Skill

1. Introduce lesson worksheet #1 (page 15). The students are asked to write action verbs on lines in a paragraph.

2. On lesson worksheet #2 (page 16), the students make lists of action verbs they would associate with different places.

3. Written Application: Have each student write a letter to a friend or relative telling about all the things he or she did on a given day. When the writing is completed, have students read their letters and list on a separate sheet of paper all of the action verbs used.

Publishing Project

Students will use their addressed, stamped envelopes from home to send their letters.

Computer Connection

Using a word processing program, create two columns on the page. Label each column with a different occupation. In a text box at the bottom of the page, type a scrambled list of action verbs associated with the occupations. Demonstrate how to copy, cut, and paste words from the list to the appropriate section of the page.

Evaluation

1. Lesson Objectives: Measure each student's progress by reviewing participation in class discussions and performance on the lesson worksheets.

2. Written Application: Use a selected rubric from pages 135–137 to evaluate progress. Record mastery on the skills checklist on pages 138 and 139. If desired, have each student use the self-assessment sheet on page 140 to evaluate his or her work.

Action Verbs

Worksheet #1

Complete the sentences to make a paragraph. Circle the action verbs.

When I wake up in the morning, I _____

_____

_____

_____.

Then I _____

_____

_____

_____.

Next I _____

_____

_____

_____.

After that I_____

_____

_____

_____.

Finally I_____

_____

_____

_____.

Action Verbs

Worksheet #2

Under each word below, write action verbs that describe what you would do there.

School

_____

_____

_____

_____

_____

_____

_____

Swimming Pool

_____

_____

_____

_____

_____

_____

_____

Home

_____

_____

_____

_____

_____

_____

Friend's House

_____

_____

_____

_____

_____

_____

Standards and Benchmarks: 1A, 1F

Strong Verbs

Using strong verbs in descriptive writing is one way authors "show" rather than "tell" their readers and increase interest in their writing. With this activity, help your students increase their vocabulary by practicing strong, specific, colorful verbs that they can use in their descriptive writing.

Goal: Students will use strong verbs to replace general, overused verbs in descriptive sentences.

Objectives

1. The student will act out the meaning of strong verbs.

2. The student will contribute to a classroom thesaurus.

3. The student will use strong verbs in writing.

4. The student will categorize synonymous verbs.

Materials

- copy of a children's thesaurus
- copies of pages 19 and 20, duplicated on heavy paper and cut into strong verb word cards
- chart paper
- marker
- copies of lesson worksheets (pages 21 and 22) for each student
- three-hole punched drawing paper for each student
- three-ring binder

Introduction

1. Begin the lesson by showing the students a children's *thesaurus*. Explain that a thesaurus is a book of words arranged in alphabetical order like a dictionary, only a thesaurus shows synonyms for words rather than definitions.

2. Read a few entries from the thesaurus as examples, making sure that the students understand the meaning of synonym.

3. Now discuss and record on chart paper some examples, such as *eat, walk, said,* and *look*. Brainstorm other words that mean almost the same thing as the verbs on the chart, but describe the actions more specifically. Add these words to the chart.

4. Ask your students to think about the subtle differences in meaning in these words and how each could be acted out. Have volunteers go to the front of the room and act out a word while the others guess which word is being portrayed.

Strong Verbs *(cont.)*

Group Activity

1. Divide the class into teams. One student from each team will serve as the actor. Secretly give each actor a verb to portray. Teams that guess the action receive a point.

2. Use the cards made from pages 19 and 20 in a learning center. To use, students sort the cards by placing the cards that say *ate, walked, said,* and *looked* in a row on the table. Next they place the remaining verb cards under their synonyms.

Reinforcing the Skill

1. On worksheet #1, direct students to use the word bank to fill in the blanks. Use worksheet #2 for additional practice, then ask volunteers to share their paragraphs. Discuss the different meanings that are created by the choice of verbs.

2. On the drawing paper, have students write a verb at the top of their pages. Next, they draw a picture showing the meaning of the word and write a sentence using the word. For a classroom thesaurus, place finished pages in a three-ring binder.

3. Written Application: Have each student write a descriptive paragraph about a family meal. Encourage students to use strong verbs to describe what people said, did, and how they ate.

Publishing Project

Display students' paragraphs on a bulletin board entitled "Eat, Devour, Gobble, Nibble."

Computer Connection

Using a spreadsheet, create a document containing overused verbs such as *go, play,* and *touch* at the tops of columns. Demonstrate how to use the tab key to move between columns. Have the students type synonyms in each column.

Evaluation

1. Lesson Objectives: Student progress and mastery measured by performance on the classroom thesaurus, lesson worksheets, and the learning center activity.

2. Written Application: Use a selected rubric from pages 135–137 to evaluate progress. Record mastery on the skills checklist on pages 138 and 139. If desired, have each student use the self-assessment sheet on page 140 to evaluate his or her work.

Strong Verb Word Cards 1

ate	**said**
walked	**looked**
gobbled	**nibbled**
devoured	**whispered**

Strong Verb Word Cards 2

roared	sighed
cried	yelled
strolled	tiptoed
paced	stomped

Strong Verbs

Worksheet #1

Write a verb on each line. Use the words in the Word Bank to help you.

1. The squirrel _____ on the nut.

2. I wanted to surprise my mom, so I _____ into the room.

3. I got mad and _____ off.

4. When I _____ my dinner, my mom said to eat slowly.

5. She _____ over her shoulder and saw the boy chasing her.

6. He _____ at the math problem for a long time.

7. My dad _____ back and forth because he was worried.

8. The girl _____ at the handsome movie star.

9. The hungry lion _____ his kill.

10. The people _____ slowly down the path.

11. The coach _____ at the players when they lost the game.

12. He _____ so no one heard him except his friend.

13. The girl _____, "I hurt my arm."

14. The lady _____, "I am so tired."

Word Bank

strolled	roared	stared
gobbled	glanced	stomped
whispered	paced	cried
tiptoed	devoured	gazed
nibbled	sighed	

Strong Verbs
Worksheet #2

Write a verb on each line. Use words from the Word Bank to help you.

When you are finished share your paragraph with a classmate.

The big, hungry lion _____ through the jungle. The hunter

_____ up as close as he could get to the lion, as he

_____ his snack of trail mix. He hid behind some

bushes and _____ at the lion. His guide

_____ ,"That is the biggest lion I have ever seen!" The

lion sniffed the air and turned and _____ at the hunter

and his guide hiding in the bushes. Suddenly the lion flopped down

on the jungle floor and

_____ the deer he

had just killed. "Let's get out of here,"

_____ the hunter. "I

don't like the way that guy eats!"

Word Bank

strolled	nibbled	sighed
gobbled	roared	stared
whispered	glanced	stomped
peeked	paced	cried
tiptoed	devoured	exclaimed

Standards and Benchmarks: 1F, 3F

Adjectives

At the primary level, students use adjectives to get beyond the simplest of sentences and add interest to their writing.

Goal: The students will use adjectives in their writing to make it more interesting and descriptive.

Objectives

1. The student will identify adjectives in classroom discussion.

2. The student will use adjectives to describe pictures.

3. The student will compose original sentences using adjectives.

Materials

- chart paper
- markers
- pictures from magazines or discarded calendars
- copy of a descriptive book, such as *On the Banks of Plum Creek* by Laura Ingalls Wilder (See the bibliography on page 141.)
- approximately 6' (2 m) of butcher paper
- crayons
- approximately 40 index cards
- hole punch
- string
- copy of lesson worksheet (page 26) for each student
- writing paper (with space for drawing)

Introduction

1. To introduce adjectives, show the students a picture and ask them to tell you about it.

2. Record student responses on the chart paper.

3. Tell the students that the words written on the chart paper are called *adjectives*. Explain that adjectives are words that are used to describe or tell about something. Stories are more interesting when the authors describe things. This helps us to form mental pictures of the story. When we are writing, we want to be sure to paint pictures with words for our readers.

Adjectives *(cont.)*

Group Activity

1. Have the students close their eyes and make mental pictures of a scene as you read to them from a descriptive story, such as Laura Ingalls Wilder's book, *On the Banks of Plum Creek.* (The chapter, "Rushes and Flags" is particularly descriptive.)

2. Ask the students what they were able to see in their minds as you read. Encourage specific and descriptive details.

3. Now brainstorm a long list of adjectives with the class. Record the adjectives on chart paper as they are mentioned. Prompt the students to suggest opposites, colors, and numbers.

4. Next, divide the butcher paper into four sections. Write one sentence in each section:

   Section 1: *The cat is eating.*

   Section 2: *The black cat is eating.*

   Section 3: *The big, black cat is eating.*

   Section 4: *The big, furry, black cat is eating.*

The cat is eating.

5. Show only one section at a time. Ask a volunteer to draw a picture on the butcher paper to illustrate the sentence. Then show the next section and have another volunteer draw a picture of the sentence. Continue in this manner for the remaining sentences.

6. Explain that the words added to each sentence are adjectives. Also point out how the pictures became more interesting and detailed as adjectives were added.

7. Introduce several simple sentences and have the students make the sentences more interesting by adding adjectives.

   The man stumbled.

   The boy threw the ball.

   The dog barked.

   The pizza smelled good.

Adjectives *(cont.)*

Extension Activity

1. Divide the class into groups of three or four. Let each group choose a calendar or magazine picture. Give each group four index cards. On each card, the groups write one adjective that describes the picture.

2. Punch a hole in the top of each card and four holes in the bottom of the picture. Using a loop of string, tie each card to the bottom of the picture. Suspend the completed adjective mobiles from the ceiling with string.

Reinforcing the Skill

1. Introduce the lesson worksheet, which requires the students to add adjectives from a word bank to simple sentences.

2. Written Application: Using writing paper, have each student draw a picture of his or her favorite toy. Then students will write three or four sentences about it (without mentioning the name of the toy), including adjectives to describe it.

Publishing Project

Display the toy descriptions on a bulletin board entitled "Guess Our Favorite Toys." Cover each picture with a half-sheet of paper labeled "Guess my favorite toy. The adjectives will help you."

Computer Connection

Using a word processing program, create a document with a word bank of adjectives. Write sentences with blanks before the nouns and have the students type appropriate adjectives in the blanks.

Evaluation

1. Lesson Objectives: Measure each student's progress by reviewing participation in class discussion and performance on the lesson worksheet and the written application.

2. Written Application: Use a selected rubric from pages 135–137 to evaluate progress. Record mastery on the skills checklist on pages 138 and 139. If desired, have each student use the self-assessment sheet on page 140 to evaluate his or her work.

Adjectives Worksheet

Add adjectives to the sentences. Use the word bank to help you.

1. The _____, _____ fire engine roared down the street.

2. The _____, _____ girl was scared.

3. The _____, _____ cat meowed softly.

4. The _____, _____ apple was good.

5. The _____, _____ bug walked across the floor.

6. The _____, _____ bird sat on the wire.

7. The _____, _____ star shone in the sky.

8. The _____, _____ clown made me laugh.

9. The _____, _____ flower smelled very good.

10. The _____, _____ chair was nice to sit in.

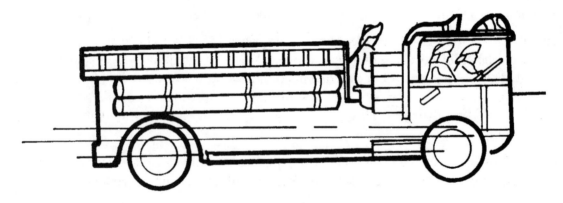

Word Bank			
beautiful	crisp	little	shy
big	fast	loud	silly
black	funny	red	soft
blue	furry	shiny	twinkling

Standards and Benchmarks: 1E, 1G

Adverbs

At the primary level, students use adverbs to tell when and how something happened.

Goal: The students will use adverbs in their writing to make it more descriptive.

Objectives

1. The student will identify the adverbs in a sentence.

2. The student will identify whether an adverb describes when or how something happened.

3. The student will use adverbs in his or her original writing.

Materials

- chart paper
- markers
- one copy of page 30; cut sentences into strips
- 1 loaf of bread
- paper towels
- plastic knives
- 1 jar of peanut butter
- 1 jar of jelly
- copies of lesson worksheets (pages 31 and 32) for each student

Introduction

1. Explain that *adverbs* are words that tell when or how something happened.

2. Write *when* and *how* at the top of the chart paper as column headings. Ask the students to name words that tell *when* such as *first, before, after, during, now, then.* Write them under the heading "when." Do the same for the word *how.* Some words that tell how are the *-ly* words such as *quickly, slowly, happily, badly, cheerfully, sadly,* and *skillfully.* Tell the students that quite often adverbs end in *-ly.*

3. Have a volunteer select one of the sentence strips made from page 30 to act out for the class. The students guess the adverb being portrayed. Repeat with the remaining sentence strips.

Adverbs *(cont.)*

Group Activity

1. Prepare for this activity by writing the following recipe on a piece of chart paper:

How to Make a Peanut Butter and Jelly Sandwich

1. Take out two pieces of bread.

2. Lay them on a paper towel.

3. Spread peanut butter on them.

4. Spread jelly on them.

5. Put them on top of each other.

---

2. Display the prepared recipe and read it with your class.

3. Discuss with students how they think the sandwich would turn out if someone who had never seen a peanut butter and jelly sandwich tried to follow those instructions.

4. Express concern that the instructions may be lacking some necessary adverbs. At this point, you can either actually demonstrate making the sandwich or you can just discuss what could happen with the students:

   1. Take out two pieces of bread.

   2. Lay them on a paper towel. *(It didn't say flat or side-by-side, so overlap them.)*

   3. Spread peanut butter on them. *(It didn't say thinly, so scoop out most of the jar and slather it on.)*

   4. Spread jelly on them. *(Same as the peanut butter.)*

   5. Put them on top of each other. *(It didn't say to put the peanut butter side down, so put it up and try to eat the mess.)*

5. Rewrite the recipe with the students adding some much-needed adverbs. Suggested revision:

How to Make a Peanut Butter and Jelly Sandwich

1. *First, take out two slices of bread.*

2. *Then, lay them side-by-side on a paper towel.*

3. *Next, thinly spread peanut butter on top of one slice.*

4. *After that, spread jelly thinly on the other slice.*

5. *Finally, keeping the peanut butter side down, place it on top of the jelly.*

Adverbs *(cont.)*

Reinforcing the Skill

1. Introduce worksheet #1 (page 31), on which the students are asked to circle the adverb in each sentence and indicate whether it tells when or how.

2. Continue practicing the skill by having the students complete worksheet #2 (page 32). They are to choose an adverb from a word bank to fix the cartoon.

3. Written Application: Have the students write a "How-to" paragraph describing a skill with which they are familiar. Remind them of the importance of adverbs when writing instructions. When finished, students can illustrate their instructions with sequential drawings.

Publishing Project

Display the How-to paragraphs on a bulletin board entitled "Find Out How To…"

Computer Connection

Using a word processing program, create a document with a list of adverbs. Instruct the students to type a sentence using each adverb.

Evaluation

1. Lesson Objectives: Measure each student's progress by reviewing performance on the lesson worksheets and the Written Application.

2. Written Application: Use a selected rubric from pages 135–137 to evaluate progress. Record mastery on the skills checklist on pages 138 and 139. If desired, have each student use the self-assessment sheet on page 140 to evaluate his or her work.

Adverbs *(cont.)*

He walked slowly.

She laughed loudly.

The boy was sadly looking out the window.

The girl smiled happily.

The dog barked angrily.

The lady played the piano softly.

The man turned the pages quickly.

The student read silently.

The runners ran fast.

The mother stirred slowly.

The girls whispered quietly.

The boy ate politely.

Adverbs

Worksheet #1

Circle the adverb in each sentence. On the line write *when* or *how*.

1. First, write your name at the top of the paper. _____

2. She danced prettily down the steps. _____

3. The flowers bloomed beautifully. _____

4. Finally, she waved good-bye. _____

5. Next, we will go to recess. _____

6. Let's play quietly so Mom can sleep. _____

7. Run quickly and tell the teacher. _____

8. Tip toe softly out of the room. _____

9. The wind blew swiftly across the lake. _____

10. We should go now. _____

11. The alarm rang loudly. _____

12. The lady sang nicely. _____

13. The man bowed politely. _____

14. Then we went home. _____

Adverbs

Worksheet #2

Use an adverb from the word bank to fix each cartoon.

1. Turn the music on
   _____.

2. Come and get me
   _____.

3. Walk past the sleeping lion
   _____.

4. Say, "Good morning,"
   _____.

5. Eat
   _____.

6. Speak
   _____.

Word Bank

politely	loudly
softly	quietly
cheerfully	soon

Standards and Benchmarks: 1C, 3I

Capitalization

At the primary level, students are required to capitalize the first word of a sentence, proper nouns, and the pronoun "I."

Goal: Students will use a capital letter for the first word of a sentence, proper nouns, and the pronoun "I."

Objectives

1. The student will identify where the capital is needed in prewritten sentences.

2. The student will use capital letters on the first word of a sentence, at the beginning of proper nouns, and for the pronoun "I."

Materials

- chart paper
- markers
- overhead transparency of page 36
- approximately 6' (2 m) of white butcher paper
- one copy of page 37, duplicated on heavy paper
- three pushpins
- hole punch
- medium-sized cardboard box
- foam packing peanuts
- copy of lesson worksheet (page 38) for each student
- pictures of dinosaurs

Introduction and Group Activity

1. Draw a line down the center of the chart paper, creating two columns. Label one column "nouns," and underneath it write *girl*. Ask the students to supply names of girls. Record the names in the second, unnamed column.

2. Repeat the process with the nouns *boy*, *school*, *restaurant*, and *store*.

3. After collecting an extensive list of proper nouns beside the common nouns, ask the students if they can tell you what is different about the words in the second column.

4. Draw the students' attention to the capital letter at the beginning of each of the words in the second column.

Capitalization *(cont.)*

Introduction and Group Activity *(cont.)*

5. Explain that names of people, places, and things are called proper nouns and begin with a capital letter. Write the title *Proper Nouns* at the top of the second column.

6. Tell the students that a proper noun is just one of the places that a capital letter is used. There are two other times that they will need to use capitals.

7. Write the following three sentences on the chart paper, omitting the beginning capitals:

    my brother likes dinosaurs.

    one of my favorite dinosaurs is triceratops.

    the triceratops has three horns on its face.

8. Read the sentences aloud with the students. Help them discover that these sentences are not correct because they do not begin with **capital letters**. Tell the students that a sentence always begins with a capital letter. Correct the sentences by adding a capital letter at the beginning of each one.

9. Review the two places they have learned to use a capital letter: in proper nouns and at the beginning of a sentence.

10. Teach capitalization of the pronoun "I" by writing the following sentences on chart paper:

    My mom and i went to the museum to see the dinosaurs.

    When i saw the triceratops, i was excited.

    In the museum store, i found a book about the triceratops.

11. Read the sentences aloud with the class. Point out the places where capitals were used correctly. Have students identify the need for capital letters in each sentence. Lead them to recognize that the pronoun "I" always needs to be capitalized.

12. Review the three places where students always need to use capital letters. Explain that you will be using the triceratops to help remember these three rules because it has three horns.

Learning Center Activity

1. To prepare, use an overhead projector to display the overhead transparency onto a butcher paper-covered bulletin board. When the illustration is the desired size, use a black marker to trace.

Capitalization *(cont.)*

Learning Center Activity *(cont.)*

2. Place a pushpin in each of the horns, and label the bulletin board "Capitalizing on Dinosaur Discovery."

3. Cut out the dinosaur bones sentence strips copied from page 37 and laminate for durability. Punch a hole in the end of each bone.

4. Place the cardboard box on a table beside the bulletin board, and fill it with the foam packing peanuts. "Bury" the bones in the packing peanuts.

5. In the center, a student "digs" for the bones. Next, he or she reads the sentence and hangs it on the horn that states the rule that will correct the sentence.

Reinforcing the Skill

1. Introduce the lesson worksheet, on which the students are asked to sort, copy, and correct capitalization errors in sentences.

2. Written Application: Display pictures of dinosaurs. Have each student write one or two sentences describing each picture.

Publishing Project

Compile the dinosaur pictures and descriptive sentences into a class book.

Computer Connection

Using a word processing program, create a paragraph using all lowercase letters. Show the students how to delete an unwanted letter, then retype the letter, pressing the shift key to capitalize it.

Evaluation

1. Lesson Objectives: Measure each student's progress by reviewing participation in the learning center, and performance on the worksheet and on the descriptive sentences.

2. Written Application: Use a selected rubric from pages 135–137 to evaluate progress. Record mastery on the skills checklist on pages 138 and 139. If desired, have each student use the self-assessment sheet on page 140 to evaluate his or her work.

Capitalization *(cont.)*

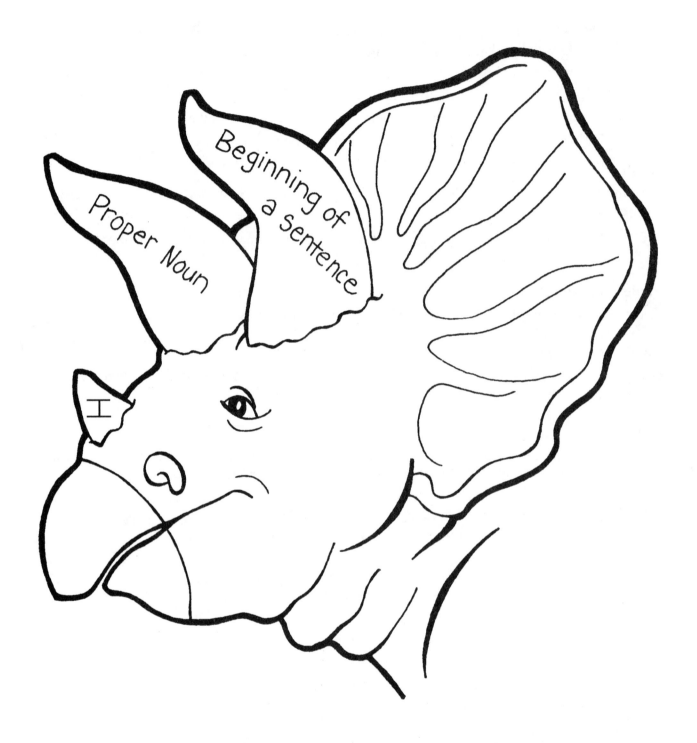

Capitalization (cont.)

Dinosaur Bones Sentence Strips

the triceratops has three horns.

My friend, christy, likes dinosaurs.

My sister and i like to read books about dinosaurs.

when we go to the museum, we will see the dinosaurs.

The triceratops is a dinosaur.

When andrew found a bone, he thought it belonged to a dinosaur.

At safeway, there was a book about dinosaurs.

Yesterday, i saw a video about the triceratops.

My mom said that i know a lot about dinosaurs.

dinosaurs are my favorite things.

at school, we learned about triceratops.

When i dig in the sand, i hope i will find a dinosaur bone.

Capitalization Worksheet

Copy each sentence on the blank lines on the triceratops's head that describes the mistake. Be sure to correct the mistakes when you copy the sentences.

digging for dinosaur bones is fun.

When i grow up, i want to hunt for dinosaurs.

I think my friends, kyle and amy like dinosaurs, too.

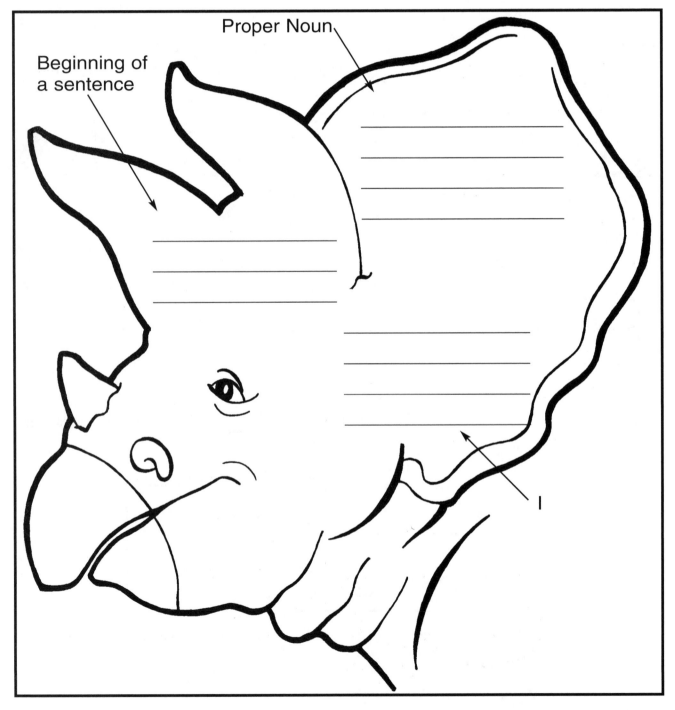

Standards and Benchmarks: 3J

End Marks

At the primary level, students need to distinguish between the four types of sentences and use the proper end mark for each.

Goal: The students will use proper end marks at the ends of statements, commands, questions, and exclamations.

Objectives

1. The student will participate in a learning center and identify the proper end mark for prewritten sentences.

2. The student will supply the proper end marks for sentences.

3. The student will use the proper end marks on original sentences.

Materials

- 1 bone (such as a chicken bone)
- chart paper
- markers
- overhead transparency of page 36
- three pushpins
- one copy of page 37

- correction fluid
- hole punch
- medium-sized cardboard box
- foam packing peanuts
- copy of lesson worksheet (page 42) for each student
- writing paper

Introduction

1. Display the chicken bone and allow the students to see it.

2. Listen as they look at the bone and record on the chart paper some of the sentences they say. Try to record at least one statement, one command, one question, and one exclamation.

End Marks *(cont.)*

Introduction *(cont.)*

3. When all of the students have had a chance to see the bone, direct their attention to the sentences you recorded on the chart paper. Discuss the types of sentences:

   A *statement sentence* tells a fact. It ends with a period.

   A *command sentence* tells someone to do something. It also ends with a period.

   A *question sentence* asks something and requires an answer. A question sentence ends with a question mark.

   An *exclamation sentence* conveys strong feeling or excitement. It ends with an exclamation mark.

Group Activity

1. Divide a sheet of chart paper into four sections. Label each section with a different heading: statements, commands, questions, and exclamations.

2. Ask the students to make statements about the bone. Record the statements in the appropriate section of the chart paper. Draw attention each time to the period at the end of the statement.

3. Continue in this manner for commands, questions, and exclamations. Assist the students in creating commands, questions, and exclamations with these prompts:

   Command: *Ask me something about the bone.*

   Question: *What should I do with this bone?*

   Exclamation: *That's a dinosaur bone!*

Learning Center Activity

1. On a bulletin board, display the triceratops head that was used in the learning center described on pages 34 and 35. Label each horn with new headings: period, question mark, and exclamation mark. As before, place a pushpin at the end of each of the triceratops's horns.

2. On the duplicate copy of page 37, use correction fluid to delete the sentences. Copy the page and cut out the bones. Program each bone with either a statement, command, question, or exclamation sentence, omitting the end marks. Laminate for durability, then punch a hole in the end of each bone.

End Marks *(cont.)*

Learning Center Activity *(cont.)*

3. Place the cardboard box on a table beside the bulletin board, and fill it with the foam packing peanuts. "Bury" the bones in the packing peanuts.

4. In the center, a student "digs" for the bones. Next, he or she reads the sentence and determines the kind of sentence and the end mark it needs. The student then hangs the bone on the correct horn.

Reinforcing the Skill

1. Introduce the lesson worksheet (page 42). The students are asked to supply end marks and identify sentence types.

2. Written Application: Have each student fold a sheet of writing paper to make four sections. The student labels each section with a different type of sentence—statement, command, question, exclamation. Have the student write three sentences in each section using the proper end mark.

Publishing Project

Have each student write a list of two or three questions about dinosaurs. Take the students to the library to check out books about dinosaurs. After the students have read the books, discuss answers to the questions. Have each student write the answers to his or her questions in statement form. Publish the questions and answers in a classroom book called "Questions and Answers About Dinosaurs."

Computer Connection

Using a word processing program, create a list of sentences (different types). Omit the end marks. Have the students insert the proper end marks.

Evaluation

1. Lesson Objectives: Measure each student's progress by reviewing participation in the learning center, and performance on the worksheet, the Written Application, and the publishing project.

2. Written Application: Use a selected rubric from pages 135–137 to evaluate progress. Record mastery on the skills checklist on pages 138 and 139. If desired, have each student use the self-assessment sheet on page 140 to evaluate his or her work.

End Marks Worksheet

Put the correct end mark in the box at the end of each sentence. Write *statement, command, question,* or *exclamation* on the line below it.

1. Triceratops lived long ago ☐

_____

2. Was triceratops the biggest dinosaur ☐

_____

3. That dinosaur looks mean, wow ☐

_____

4. Get away from there ☐

_____

5. Give him some food ☐

_____

6. Where did the triceratops live ☐

_____

7. How long is his tail ☐

_____

8. Some dinosaurs laid eggs ☐

_____

9. Let me see the bone ☐

_____

10. That dinosaur has three sharp horns, wow ☐

_____

11. Please help me ☐

_____

12. The dinosaurs roamed the earth ☐

_____

Standards and Benchmarks: 1C, 1F, 1H, 3B

Complete Sentences

Writing complete sentences is a basic skill that needs to be emphasized at the primary level to develop correct writing habits.

Goal: The students will use complete sentences in their original writing.

Objectives

1. The students will distinguish between complete and incomplete sentences.

2. The students write complete sentences on a worksheet.

3. The students will use complete sentences in their own writing.

Materials

- copy of page 46, cut into subject/predicate cards
- elephant patterns (page 47)
- copy of page 48, cut into sentence strips
- blank sentence strip for each student
- hole punch
- scissors
- glue
- colored construction paper
- string (for each student, you will need a 3' piece and two 6" pieces)
- one drinking straw for each student
- copy of lesson worksheet (page 49) for each student
- picture from magazines or discarded calendar for each student
- writing paper (with space for picture)

Group Activity

1. Give one subject/predicate card to each student. Explain that each card has only one half of a sentence on it. Help the students read the cards. Explain that one card is not a complete idea. It does not seem finished.

2. Instruct students to find the classmate that has the other half of their sentence on his or her card. When they have found the other half of their sentences, have the students sit down with their partners.

3. Demonstrate that the sentences are now complete by asking the partners to read their cards to the class.

Complete Sentences *(cont.)*

Group Activity *(cont.)*

4. Explain that a sentence tells about someone or something and what happens. A sentence must have a noun and a verb. The noun is called the subject and the verb is called the predicate. (Remind students that a complete sentence always starts with a capital letter and ends with an end mark.)

5. Collect the subject and predicate cards. Randomly read the cards aloud, sometimes reading just one part and sometimes reading the complete sentence. Have the students give a "thumbs up" if they hear a complete sentence, or "thumbs down" if not. Add some other phrases such as:

in the lake
across the field
down the street
in the garden
the big, shiny fish
the little baby
the old man
the red and blue striped ball
swam slowly
cried loudly
galloped rapidly
blew very hard

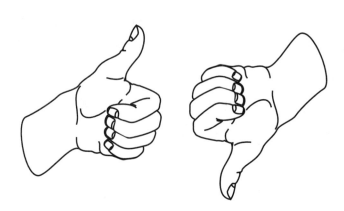

Learning Center Activity

1. Using the subject/predicate cards in a center, allow the students to put the subjects and predicates together randomly to make silly sentences. Have students illustrate the silly sentences; then bind them together to make a "Silly Sentences Book."

2. For a different center, cut out the elephant patterns from a copy of page 47, and place them in the center along with the sentence cards made from page 48. To participate in the center, a student will sort the cards as follows: the cards that have complete sentences are placed below the "complete" elephant and the cards that do not have complete sentences are placed below the "incomplete" elephant.

Extension Activity

1. Make a sentence mobile. Instruct students to write a complete sentence on the sentence strip. Then cut the sentence into two pieces between the subject and the predicate.

Complete Sentences *(cont.)*

Extension Activity *(cont.)*

2. Glue each piece onto colored construction paper that has been cut into a desired shape, preferably a shape that illustrates the sentence.

3. Punch a hole at the top of each sentence part.

4. Tie the longer piece of string to the center of the drinking straw.

5. Tie each of the two shorter pieces of string to a sentence part. Tie the opposite ends to the ends of the straw. Hang the mobiles above the students' desks.

Reinforcing the Skill

1. Introduce the lesson worksheet, which asks students to write in the blanks to make a complete sentence.

2. Written Application: Display the calendar or magazine pictures, and allow each student to choose one that he or she likes. After gluing the picture to the writing paper, the student then writes complete sentences that describe the picture.

Publishing Project

Display the students' writing on a bulletin board entitled "We Use Complete Sentences."

Computer Connection

Using a word processing program, create a document with sentence subjects in one text box and sentence predicates in another text box. A student chooses a subject from one box and a predicate from the other, then will copy, cut, and paste the parts to create a complete sentence.

Evaluation

1. Lesson Objectives: Measure each student's progress by reviewing participation in the learning center and performance on the mobile, the lesson worksheet, and the Written Application.

2. Written Application: Use your choice of rubrics from pages 135–137 to evaluate each student's written work. Based on the rubric score, determine the need for reteaching or further practice. Record skills mastery on the checklist on pages 138 and 139. If desired, have each student evaluate his or her own work using the self-assessment sheet on page 140.

Complete Sentences *(cont.)*

Subject/Predicate Cards

Subject *(noun)* The fish	**Predicate** *(verb)* swam.	**Subject** *(noun)* The baby
Predicate *(verb)* cried.	**Subject** *(noun)* The horse	**Predicate** *(verb)* galloped.
Subject *(noun)* The wind	**Predicate** *(verb)* blew.	**Subject** *(noun)* The ice cream
Predicate *(verb)* melted.	**Subject** *(noun)* The dog	**Predicate** *(verb)* barked.
Subject *(noun)* The bird	**Predicate** *(verb)* flew.	**Subject** *(noun)* The pizza
Predicate *(verb)* smelled good.	**Subject** *(noun)* The boy	**Predicate** *(verb)* felt sad.
Subject *(noun)* The man	**Predicate** *(verb)* sneezed.	**Subject** *(noun)* The ball
Predicate *(verb)* bounced.	**Subject** *(noun)* The flowers	**Predicate** *(verb)* bloomed.

Complete Sentences *(cont.)*

Sentence Strips

The big, orange fish

swam in the lake.

The little baby

cried very loudly for a long time.

The beautiful, golden horse

galloped across the field.

The big, black dog

barked at me.

The bird

flew up in the tree.

The ball

bounced away from me.

The colorful flowers

bloomed by the gate.

My ice cream

melted because the sun was hot.

Complete Sentences *(cont.)*

Complete Sentences

Incomplete Sentences

Complete Sentences Worksheet

Write on the lines to make complete sentences.

1. The girl _____.

2. _____ walked down the street.

3. _____ played in the park.

4. The little, black dog _____.

5. _____ went to the movies.

6. _____ blew in the wind.

7. Every apple on the tree _____.

8. _____ laughed and clapped for the clown.

9. All the students in our class _____.

10. My mom and dad _____.

11. _____ yelled very loud.

12. At the ballgame, the boys _____.

13. After lunch, we _____.

14. _____ play with the jump rope.

Standards and Benchmarks: 1A, 1F

Narrowing the Topic

Students at the primary level often choose much too broad a topic to write about, making their writing general, containing few details. Narrowing the topic can help relieve these problems and greatly improve the product.

Goal: The students will narrow topics and use more detail and description.

Objectives

1. The student will participate in a class discussion about narrowing broad topics.

2. The student will choose a narrow topic and write a descriptive paragraph.

Materials

- set of encyclopedias
- one copy of page 53, mounted on tag board and laminated
- erasable marker
- multiple copies (4 per student) of "Topic Triangle" (page 53)

Introduction

1. Tell the students that good writing usually has lots of details to paint word pictures for the reader. If a topic is too broad, it is difficult to use the necessary details. In order to improve writing, it is important to learn to *narrow the topic*.

2. Show the students an encyclopedia article on a broad topic, *animals*. Thumb through the pages to demonstrate the length of the article. Read some of the related topics given for that article.

3. Ask the students to think of a topic that would be narrower and easier to write about. Suggest a specific animal topic, such as *dogs*. Show the article in the encyclopedia and come to the conclusion that "dogs" is still a very broad topic.

4. Suggest a particular breed of dog, such as *golden retriever*. Again show the encyclopedia article on that narrower topic and guide students to the conclusion that this topic still might be too broad.

5. Ask how the topic could be narrowed even more. Suggest a *certain golden retriever that you know*. Now the topic is becoming manageable. However, to write a paragraph about a certain dog, it might be best to focus on an interesting occurrence with the dog, for example, "The time my golden retriever got out of the yard."

Narrowing the Topic *(cont.)*

Group Activity

1. Using an erasable marker, write *Animals* at the bottom of the laminated Topic Triangle. In the next space above, write *Dogs*. Above that, write *Golden Retrievers*, then *My Dog*, and in the apex of the triangle, write *The time my golden retriever got out of the yard.*

2. To prepare for this part of the activity, choose some of the following broad topics to write on slips of scratch paper:

birds	*movies*
flowers	*games*
cities	*pets*
insects	*computers*
trips	*teachers*
amusement parks	*restaurants*
school	*rivers*
trees	*mountains*
books	*hobbies*
sports	*horses*
cooking	*houses*
holidays	*feelings*
television	

3. Ask a volunteer to select a broad topic slip. Then work together with the class to create narrower and narrower topics until reaching a more specific one. Continue in this manner for several more topics.

Reinforcing the Skill

1. Provide each student with three Topic Triangles. Write a list of broad topics (e.g., Vacations, School, Families) on the chalkboard. For each Topic Triangle, the student selects a broad topic and narrows it to result in a specific writing topic. Then have the student write a paragraph for each narrowed topic.

2. Written Application: Provide the students with a broad topic and have them complete a Topic Triangle, narrowing it to a topic appropriate for writing one paragraph. Instruct each student to write about the narrowed topic.

Narrowing the Topic *(cont.)*

Publishing Project

Display the paragraphs on a bulletin board entitled "Getting Specific."

Computer Connection

1. Allow students to explore information using a CD-ROM encyclopedia. Have each student do a search on a broad topic of interest and narrow it farther and farther. Students write the results of their search on a Topic Triangle.

2. Have each student report to the class about the original topic and how it was narrowed.

Evaluation

1. Lesson Objectives: Measure each student's progress by reviewing performance on the lesson worksheet and the Written Application.

2. Written Application: Use your choice of rubrics from pages 135–137 to evaluate each student's written work. Based on the rubric score, determine the need for reteaching or further practice. Record skills mastery on the checklist on pages 138 and 139. If desired, have each student evaluate his or her own work using the self-assessment sheet on page 140.

Topic Triangle

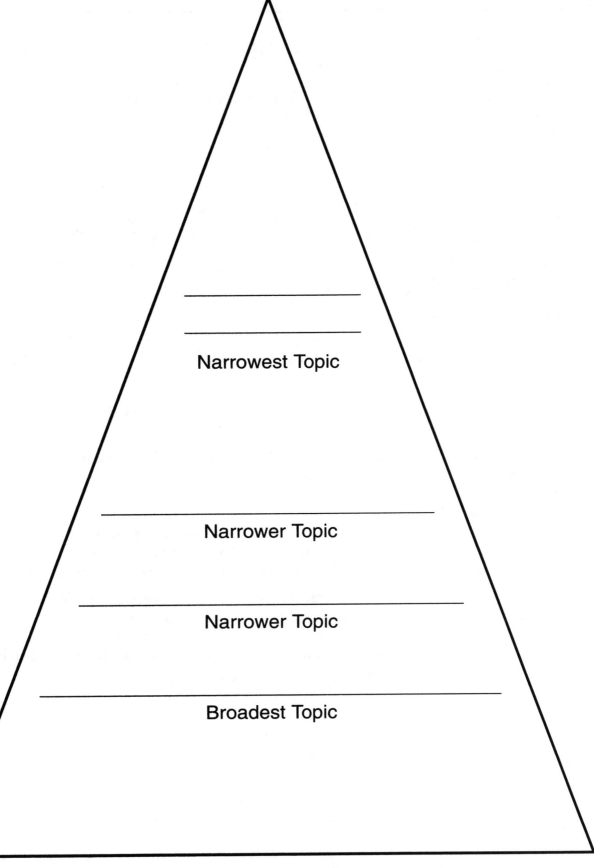

Narrowest Topic

Narrower Topic

Narrower Topic

Broadest Topic

Standards and Benchmarks: 1C, 3A, 3B, 3H

Spelling

Students at the primary level are expected to spell high frequency words and use a dictionary to spell words. This lesson will help your students correct their spelling using a simple dictionary.

Goal: Students will correctly spell high-frequency words.

Objectives

1. The student will practice putting words in alphabetical order.

2. The student will use a simple dictionary to identify the correct spelling of high-frequency words.

Materials

- copies of pages 56–59 for each student
- scissors
- stapler
- copies of lesson worksheets (pages 60–62) for each student

Introduction

1. Explain to your students that it is important to use *correct spelling* in writing. Using correct spelling helps a person to easily read the work.

2. Review with students that a dictionary is a helpful resource for spelling words correctly. Words in a dictionary are placed in alphabetical order.

Group Activity

1. This activity provides practice in placing words in alphabetical order. Write five words on the chalkboard, such as *mat, box, cat, five,* and *tree*. Underline the first letter of each word. Then have the students identify the letter that would come first in ABC order. Write the list in order.

2. Write three more words on the chalkboard that begin with the same letter, such as *blend, bat,* and *beg*. Draw the students' attention to the first letter of each word and ask, "How do we put words in ABC order if they begin with the same letter?" Explain that putting these words in order requires looking at the second letter of each word. Underline the second letters and then have the students place the words in order.

Spelling *(cont.)*

Reinforcing the Skill

1. Introduce the lesson worksheet #1. The students are asked to write each set of words in alphabetical order. Explain to students that the words on the lower portion of the page need to be alphabetized by the second letter of the words.

2. To assemble a *My Book of Words* dictionary, each student cuts apart the pages, stacks them in order, and staples them together along the left edge.

3. When the dictionaries have been assembled, write the word *then* on the chalkboard. Ask, "What letter is at the beginning of the word?" Then have the students find the **T** section of their dictionaries. After finding the section, have them look through the list to find the word.

4. Provide each student with a copy of lesson worksheet #2 to locate certain words in the *My Book of Words* booklet.

5. Lesson worksheet #3 contains a passage of text with numerous misspellings of high-frequency words. The student identifies each misspelling, locates it in the word booklet, and writes the correct spelling above the word in the text.

6. Written Application: Have each student write a story about a desired topic. While writing, instruct the student to use his or her dictionary to help with spelling.

Publishing Project

1. Divide the class into pairs and have them edit each other's letters. Encourage the students to use their dictionaries to check word spelling.

Evaluation

1. Lesson Objectives: Measure progress by reviewing each student's participation in the group activity and the lesson worksheet.

2. Written Application: Check each student's ability to use the dictionary to correctly spell high-frequency words. Use your choice of rubrics from pages 135–137 to evaluate each student's written work. Based on the rubric score, determine the need for reteaching or further practice. Record skills mastery on the checklist on pages 138 and 139. If desired, have each student evaluate his or her own work using the self-assessment sheet on page 140.

Spelling *(cont.)*

My Book of Words

Name: _____

A

about

after

all

am

an

and

are

as

at

_____

_____

_____

Page 1

B

back

be

because

been

big

but

by

_____

_____

_____

Page 2

C

came

come

could

_____

D

day

did

_____

E

eagle

edge

_____

Page 3

Spelling *(cont.)*

F

first
for
from

_____

_____

G

get
go
going
got

_____

_____

Page 4

H

had
has
have
he
her
here
him
his

_____

_____

Page 5

I

if
into
is
it

_____

_____

J

joke
jumped
just

_____

_____

Page 6

K

king
knee

_____

_____

L

like
little
look

_____

_____

Page 7

Spelling *(cont.)*

M
made
make
me
more
my

_____

_____

N
no
not
now

_____

_____

Page 8

O
of
off
on
one
or
our
out
over

_____

P
pack
peace
pick
pretty

_____

Page 9

Q
quarter
queen
quit

_____

_____

R
raccoon
rain
rent
ring

_____

_____

Page 10

S
said
saw
see
she
so
some

_____

_____

Page 11

Spelling *(cont.)*

T

that

the

their

them

then

there

they

this

to

two

_____

_____

Page 12

U

under

up

use

_____

_____

V

van

very

view

visit

voice

_____

_____

Page 13

W

was

we

well

went

were

what

when

where

who

will

with

would

_____

_____

Page 14

X

Y

yard

year

yet

you

your

_____

Z

zebra

zero

zip

zoo

_____

Page 15

Spelling

Worksheet #1

Write each group of words in alphabetical order. Check your answers using your word booklet.

did   _____

down   _____

day   _____

to   _____

then   _____

two   _____

our   _____

only   _____

off   _____

Write each group of words in ABC order. (Hint: Look at the second or third letter of each word.)

has   _____

had   _____

have   _____

went   _____

would   _____

will   _____

saw   _____

some   _____

see   _____

Spelling

Worksheet #2

Find each word below in your word booklet. Write the words that come before and after each one.

1. _____ are _____

2. _____ because _____

3. _____ here _____

4. _____ little _____

5. _____ will _____

6. _____ there _____

7. _____ she _____

8. _____ not _____

9. _____ more _____

10. _____ into _____

11. _____ for _____

12. _____ going _____

13. _____ on _____

14. _____ what _____

Spelling

Worksheet #3

The underlined words are misspelled. Find each word in your word booklet. Write the correct spelling above each word.

Wen I was littl I did not lik to eat vegetables. My mom woud try vry hard to mak me eat them. Shee sed I needed to eat vegetables so I coold grow strong. I didn't care. I still didn't want to eat thm. Now I am older and I hav learned to like some vegetables. I wil eat salads and broccoli. Mi mom says shee is proud of me. Wen I grow up, I'm goin to be healthy and strong.

On the lines below, write about the vegetables you do and do not like. Check your word booklet for correct spelling.

_____

_____

_____

_____

_____

_____

Standards and Benchmarks: 1A, 1B, 1C, 1D

Graphic Organizers

Goal: The students will use graphic organizers to plan their descriptive writing.

Objectives

1. The student will recognize a graphic organizer (word web).
2. The student will use a graphic organizer to plan descriptive writing.

Materials

- chart paper
- marker
- copy of word web (page 65) for each student
- several copies of flow chart for advanced students (page 66)

Introduction

1. On a sheet of chart paper, draw a word web (page 65).
2. Tell your students that before starting to write, it is important to think about what will be written and the kinds of details that will be used. Explain that a *word web* can be used to plan a story or other writing piece before actually writing it.

Group Activity

1. Select a familiar topic, such as pizza. Write the topic in the center of the web. In the surrounding circles, write headings, such as *looks, tastes, smells, feels.*
2. For each of the headings, ask the students to brainstorm words or phrases that describe the topic as you write their responses around the corresponding circles.

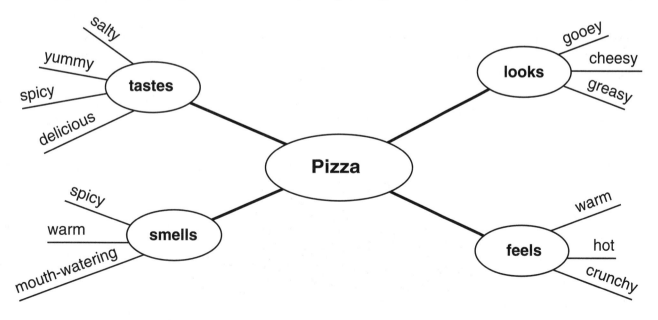

Graphic Organizers *(cont.)*

Group Activity *(cont.)*

3. As a class, write a descriptive paragraph.

   Pizza is my favorite food. It looks cheesy and gooey. It smells spicy and mouth-watering. I love to bite into the crunchy crust and taste the warm toppings.

Reinforcing the Skill

1. Distribute copies of the Word Web (page 65). Have each student select a topic and write it in the center circle. Next, add a different heading in each of the remaining circles. The page is completed with adjectives to use in a descriptive paragraph.

2. The flow chart may be a bit more difficult because it requires that students brainstorm details in sequence. Provide able students with copies of the flow chart worksheet to experiment with this type of graphic organizer.

3. Written Application: Students use their word web or flow chart to plan and write a paragraph, using as many of the brainstormed adjectives as possible.

Publishing Project

1. Pair up students to edit and revise their paragraphs.

2. Display each student's completed paragraph and graphic organizer on a bulletin board entitled "Organize Your Thoughts."

Computer Connection

Show the students how to use a computer drawing program to create a word web or flow chart using circles, squares, and lines.

Evaluation

1. Lesson Objectives: Measure progress by reviewing each student's participation in the group activity and ability to complete a word web or flow chart.

2. Written Application: Review each student's paragraph for use of descriptive words used on the graphic organizer. Use your choice of rubrics from pages 135–137 to evaluate each student's written work. Record skills mastery on the checklist on pages 138 and 139. If desired, have each student evaluate his or her own work using the self-assessment sheet on page 140.

Word Web

Flow Chart

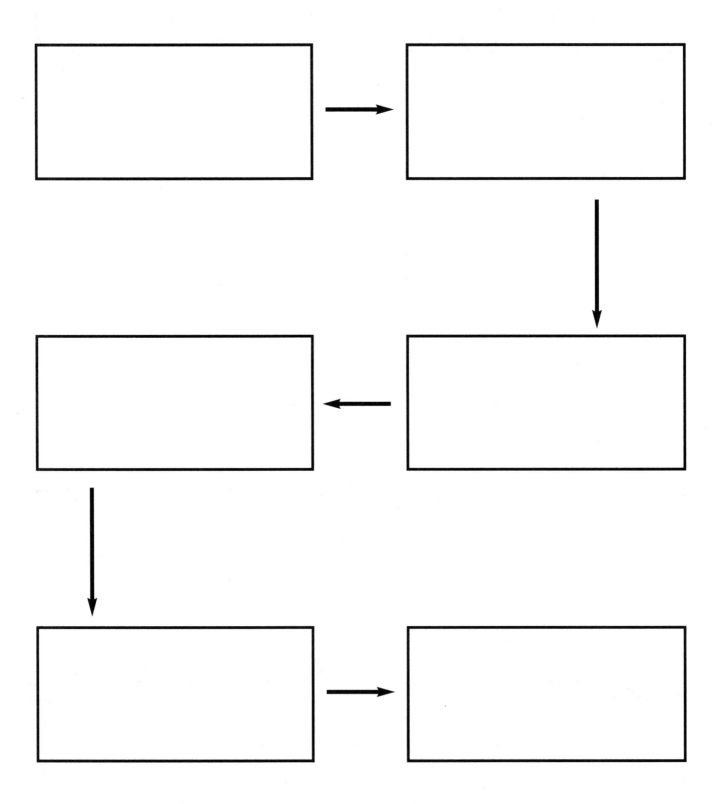

66

Standards and Benchmarks: 1F, 3F

Describing a Common Object

Goal: The students will use an object's attributes to describe it in writing.

Objectives

1. The student will practice describing objects, orally.

2. The student will write descriptions of objects for a guessing game.

3. The student will describe a favorite toy in a paragraph.

Materials

- a bag or a box with a lid to be used as a grab bag
- supply of common objects, such as:
    - —sand paper
    - —cheese grater
    - —nail
    - —hammer
    - —shoe
    - —postage stamp
    - —baby bottle
    - —dog biscuit
    - —belt
    - —pencil
- pictures of objects from magazines or discarded calendars
- an index card for each student
- copy of lesson worksheet (page 69) for each student

Introduction and Group Activity

1. Explain to the students that when they describe an object they are using the object's attributes. Attributes are the object's size, shape, color, feel, smell, sound, and use.

2. Ask for a volunteer to secretly select an object from the grab bag. The student describes the object's attributes to classmates.

Learning Center Activity

1. Distribute a magazine or calendar picture of an object. Have each student write a description of the picture on an index card. Encourage students to use as many of the object's attributes as possible.

Describing a Common Object *(cont.)*

Learning Center Activity *(cont.)*

2. When the descriptions are finished, place them in a center with the pictures for a game called "What Am I?" (To make this game self-correcting, number each picture and have students write the matching number on the back of their index cards.)

3. To play the game, students match the pictures to their descriptions.

Extension Activity

1. Ask students to bring a favorite toy from home.

2. Instruct each student to write a paragraph describing the toy.

3. When the paragraphs are complete, display all of the toys at the front of the room. Read a description and have the students decide which toy the paragraph is describing.

Reinforcing the Skill

1. Introduce the lesson worksheet. The students write words from a word bank to complete descriptive sentences.

2. Written Application: Instruct each student to write a description of a room at home and draw a picture of the room. Tell the students to include as many details as they can remember. Remind them that everything included in the picture must also be described in the paragraph.

Publishing Project

Display the pictures and paragraphs from the Written Application on a bulletin board entitled "Knock, Knock, What's in My Home?"

Evaluation

1. Lesson Objectives: Measure each student's progress by reviewing participation in the class guessing games, the center, and performance on the lesson worksheet.

2. Written Application: Use your choice of rubrics from pages 135–137 to evaluate each student's written work. Based on the rubric score, determine the need for reteaching or further practice. Record skills mastery on the checklist on pages 138 and 139. If desired, have each student evaluate his or her own work using the self-assessment sheet on page 140.

Describing a Common Object
Lesson Worksheet

Write a word from the word bank that matches the description in the sentence.

1. The tall, green leafy _____ was swaying in the wind.

2. The furry, black _____ curled up in the sunshine and slept.

3. I love to eat spicy, warm, delicious, homemade _____.

4. My _____ goes clickety clack as I roll down the street.

5. My _____ feel scratchy and red after I swim in the pool.

6. The big, soft, comfy _____ looked great when I was sleepy.

7. These old, dirty, worn out _____ need to be thrown away.

8. The happy, blue-eyed _____ sang a joyful song.

9. The warm, crackling _____ feels good on a cool night.

10. The beautiful, blue _____ stretched above us.

Word Bank

apple pie	kitten
student	sky
eyes	fire
tree	skateboard
bed	shoes

Standards and Benchmarks: 1A, 1B, 1C, 1D, 1F, 3B, 3H, 3I, 3J

Describing a Person

Goal: The students will write descriptive paragraphs about people.

Objective: The student will interview a classmate to compile information to write a description.

Materials

- hand mirrors
- drawing paper
- crayons
- two copies of page 72 for each student
- copies of pages 73 and 74 for each student

Introduction

1. Begin the lesson by giving each student a hand mirror, drawing paper, and crayons.

2. Have the students look at themselves very carefully in the mirror and draw self-portraits.

3. When the portraits are completed, ask volunteers to share their portraits with the class. As the portraits are shared, ask each artist if the portrait shows everything there is to know about him or her or if there are other things he or she could tell the class. Also, ask the class if they know anything else about each person.

4. Explain that the portrait shows the physical attributes of the person, but there are other characteristics about each person that cannot be seen in a picture. These are attributes such as personality, likes and dislikes, age, family, friends, accomplishments, hopes, dreams, and wishes. When describing a person in writing, we can be more descriptive than with just a picture.

5. Introduce worksheet #1. Read the questions aloud with the students.

Group Activity

1. To prepare for this activity, complete a copy of worksheet #1 about a fictional person.

Describing a Person *(cont.)*

Group Activity *(cont.)*

2. Ask students to partner up with a classmate for an interview. After the interviews are complete, demonstrate how to turn the information on your prepared worksheet into a paragraph about the person.

3. Instruct each student to write a paragraph about the person he or she interviewed using the information on worksheet #1.

4. Have the partners exchange paragraphs so that each student is reviewing the paragraph about himself or herself.

5. Introduce worksheet #2. This page is a revising and editing guide. Have each student revise and edit the paragraph about himself or herself. Return it to the partner who wrote it to make corrections.

Extension Activity

1. Use the frame border on page 74 to frame the self-portraits. The students cut them out and decorate as desired.

2. Display descriptive paragraphs with the self-portraits on a bulletin board entitled "Meet Our Class."

3. Written Application: Supply each student with another copy of worksheet #1. Have each student take the paper home and interview someone he or she thinks is interesting. Assign each student to write a paragraph about the interviewee.

Publishing Project

Bind the writing application paragraphs into a classroom book entitled "Interesting People We Know."

Evaluation

1. Lesson Objectives: Measure each student's progress by reviewing performance on lesson worksheets #1 and #2 and the paragraphs written.

2. Written Application: Use your choice of rubrics from pages 135–137 to evaluate each student's written work. Based on the rubric score, determine the need for reteaching or further practice. Record skills mastery on the checklist on pages 138 and 139. If desired, have each student evaluate his or her own work using the self-assessment sheet on page 140.

Describing a Person
Worksheet #1

Ask your partner these questions. Write his or her answer in the space.

1. What is your full name? _____

2. How old are you? _____

3. How many brothers and sisters do you have? _____

4. What are their names? _____

5. What do you most like to do? _____

   _____

6. What do you least like to do? _____

   _____

7. Who do you like to play with? _____

   _____

8. What do you play with friends? _____

   _____

9. What do you want to be when you grow up and why? _____

   _____

10. What chores do you do at home? _____

    _____

11. What pets do you have? _____

12. What do you remember that was the most fun you ever had?
    Tell all about it.

    _____

    _____

Describing a Person

Worksheet #2

Your name: _____

Your partner's name: _____

Read the paragraph your partner wrote about you. Answer these questions.

1. Are all of the sentences complete? If not, **circle** the sentences your partner needs to fix.

2. Did your partner start each sentence with a capital letter? If not, **underline three times** each letter that needs to be capitalized.

3. Is there a period at the end of each sentence? If not, put a **circle with a period** in it at the end of the sentence.

4. Are the proper nouns capitalized? If not, **underline three times** each letter that needs to be capitalized.

5. Are there any misspelled words? **Circle** them.

6. Did your partner get the facts right? If not, what is wrong?

_____

7. Is there anything else you would change to make this paragraph better?

_____

Proofreading Marks

Add a letter or word.	⌄
Add a space.	#
Add a punctuation mark.	⊙ ⌃
Take out something.	ℓ
Make a capital letter.	≡
Make a lowercase letter.	⁄ℓc
Word is spelled wrong.	**sp.**

Self-Portrait

Standards and Benchmarks: 1D, 1F

Details

At the primary level, students begin to add relevant details to their writing to add interest and paint word pictures.

Goal: The students will use relevant details in their writing.

Objectives

1. The student will distinguish between details and main ideas in a class discussion.

2. The student will identify relevant details.

3. The student will choose relevant details to add to original writing.

Materials

- copy of car pattern sheet (page 78), cut apart for demonstration purposes
- glue
- chart paper
- markers
- writing paper
- black butcher paper (the length of a bulletin board)
- copy of car pattern sheet (page 78) for each student
- copy of lesson worksheet (page 79) for each student

Introduction

1. Explain that writing a descriptive paragraph is like taking a reader on a trip. When the reader begins to read, he or she knows nothing about what you have written. You want to take them from knowing nothing about what you have written all the way down the road to where they know what you are trying to tell them.

2. The main idea is like a car. The reader gets into the car to go on the trip (show the main idea car). The car cannot get anywhere without tires. The tires are like the *details* the author uses to help his reader along on the trip (show the detail tires).

3. On the car write the main idea, *Going to Grandma's house is fun.*

4. Have the students give you detail sentences that support the idea that going to Grandma's house is fun. Write one detail sentence on each of four tires and glue them to the car.

5. Repeat steps 3 and 4, using main ideas such as:

    Pizza tastes delicious.

    We work hard at school.

    My dad is special.

Details *(cont.)*

Introduction *(cont.)*

6. Using the chart paper, demonstrate how to use the information on the car to write a paragraph. Show the students how to indent, write the main idea as the topic sentence, and follow it with the detail sentences.

7. The details have to be related to the main idea because unrelated details are like giving the car a flat tire. A flat tire only takes up time and doesn't help get the car where you want it to go. For example, using the main idea, "Going to Grandma's house is fun," the writer would not include "Every time I go to Grandma's, she makes me eat spinach for dinner and I hate spinach." This detail does not show that going to Grandma's house is fun. Stress that the students choose their details carefully.

Group Activity

1. Give each student a copy of the car pattern sheet. Have them write the main idea, *Recess is fun,* on his or her car. Each student will write four details—one on each of the tires. Remind them that the details need to support the main idea.

2. Encourage the students to share their details with partners. Tell the partners to be sure and check for unrelated details. These "flat tires" need to be changed by the author.

3. Have the students color and cut out their cars and glue the tires to the cars.

4. Have each student change the information on his or her car into paragraph form on the lined writing paper.

5. Prepare a bulletin board entitled "Main Ideas and Details." Using a length of black butcher paper, make a road from one side of the board to the other. Display the cars and paragraphs on the road.

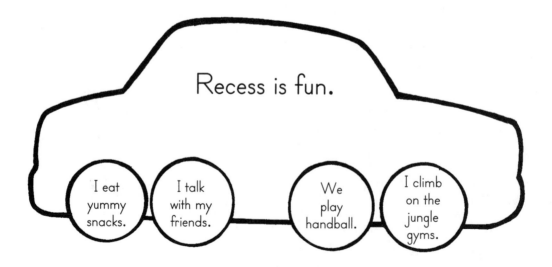

Details *(cont.)*

Reinforcing the Skill

1. Introduce the lesson worksheet, which gives the students practice in choosing related details, and writing paragraphs.

2. Written Application: Have each student personalize the main idea below, writing detail sentences to complete a paragraph.

   My favorite video is _____.

Publishing Project

Bind the students' paragraphs about their favorite videos into a classroom video review booklet.

Computer Connection

Using a word processing program, create a document with several paragraphs about different main ideas. Include in each paragraph a sentence or two that does not support the main idea. Have the students proofread the paragraphs and delete the inappropriate sentences.

Evaluation

1. Lesson Objectives: Measure each student's progress by reviewing participation in class discussion and the paragraphs written in the lesson. Also review the work on the lesson worksheet.

2. Written Application: Use your choice of rubrics from pages 135–137 to evaluate each student's written work. Based on the rubric score, determine the need for reteaching or further practice. Record skills mastery on the checklist on pages 138 and 139. If desired, have each student evaluate his or her own work using the self-assessment sheet on page 140.

Car Pattern

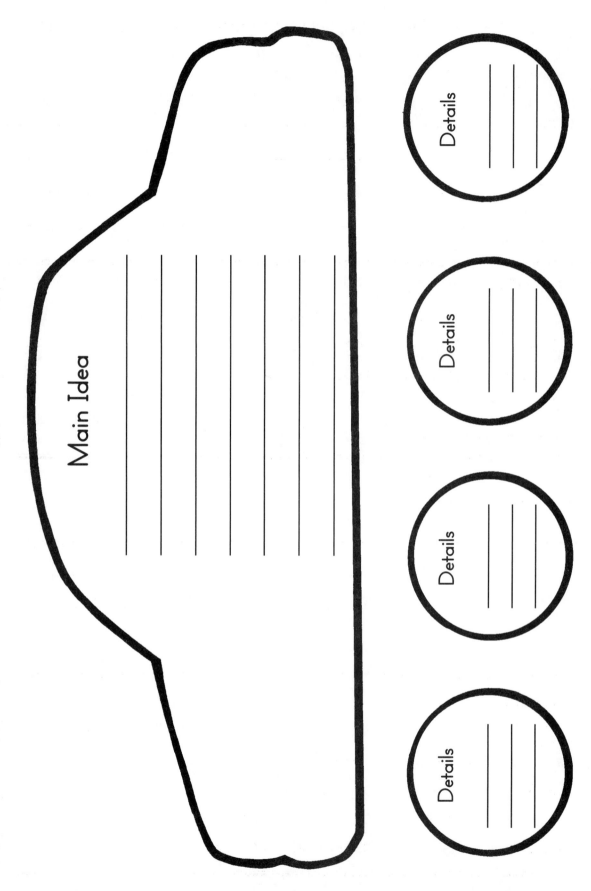

Main Idea

Details

Details

Details

Details

Details Worksheet

Support the main ideas below. Copy two or more sentences from the box below.

My sister is funny.

_____

_____

_____

_____

Details

She wears the strangest clothes I have ever seen.

She never does her homework.

She is nice to my brother.

She loves pizza.

My sister even dyed her hair blue.

I love to watch my mother cook.

_____

_____

_____

_____

Details

When she cooks bacon the fat snaps up and burns me.

Everything she makes smells so good.

Sometimes she lets me lick the bowl.

She gives me little bites of my favorite foods.

I am learning to be a good cook by watching her.

Standards and Benchmarks: 1B, 1C, 1D, 1F

Visual Images

The aim of descriptive writing is to produce vivid mental images for the reader.

Goal: The students will revise and edit a descriptive paragraph that creates a vivid mental image for the reader.

Objectives

1. The student will write a paragraph about his or her favorite animal.

2. The student will participate in a class discussion about descriptive writing.

3. The student will revise, edit, and rewrite his or her paragraph improving upon description.

Materials

- chart paper
- markers
- copies of pages 82–84 for each student

Introduction

1. To begin the lesson, have each student write a paragraph about his or her favorite animal. When the writing is complete, gather the students together with their paragraphs.

2. Ask volunteers to read their paragraphs and ask the listeners to try to visualize what the writer is describing.

3. Now lead the class in a discussion of tools they have learned about that make vivid word pictures for readers. Record the students' suggestions on the chart paper. The list should include adjectives, adverbs, strong verbs, details, and similes. Briefly review the use of each of these tools with the students.

Group Activity

1. Copy the two stories on page 82 onto chart paper for reference and distribute copies of the page to students.

2. Read the first story out loud with the students. Ask students to try to visualize what they hear.

Visual Images *(cont.)*

Group Activity *(cont.)*

3. Now read the second story, again asking students to visualize what is being read. Ask, "In which story were you able to make more vivid mental pictures?"

4. Re-read the second story, sentence by sentence, comparing it to the first story. Discuss what tools the author used to make the second story more descriptive.

Reinforcing the Skill

1. On worksheet #1, students answer questions about the paragraphs they wrote in the Introduction, Step 1 (page 80).

2. When finished, students will exchange papers with a partner and go through the same process on the partner's paper.

3. Introduce worksheet #2, which is an editing worksheet. Students will edit their original paragraphs, then rewrite them, incorporating suggestions from the two worksheets.

4. Written Application: Have each student write a descriptive paragraph about an amusement park attraction or carnival ride they have enjoyed. Remind them to use the tools listed in the Group Activity in order to write descriptively.

Publishing Project

Display the students' paragraphs on a bulletin board entitled "Fun and Scary Rides."

Computer Connection

Using a word processing program, create a document that contains a descriptive paragraph that needs revising. Demonstrate how to place the cursor between words, then delete and retype words to make the paragraph more descriptive.

Evaluation

1. Lesson Objectives: Measure each student's progress by reviewing the improvement on the paragraphs about their favorite animals. Also review the Written Application assignment.

2. Written Application: Use a selected rubric from pages 135–137 to evaluate progress. Record mastery on the skills checklist on pages 138 and 139. If desired, have each student use the self-assessment sheet on page 140 to evaluate his or her work.

Visual Images

═══ Story #1 ═══

I have a cat. Her name is Blacky. She loves me, and I love her. Blacky sits in the sun. She left one night and didn't come back for a whole week. Then she came back, and I was happy.

═══ Story #2 ═══

I have a cat that is as black as midnight so I named her Blacky. Blacky has long soft fur that tickles my nose when she sleeps curled up around my neck at night. Her soft, little meow sounds like, "I love you, Jill," to me. Blacky spends the day relaxing in the sun that comes through my bedroom window as warm as cookies right out of the oven.

One lonely night she walked out the door like she does every night. That night was different. In the morning, she was not purring on my pillow. I searched for a whole week. Every morning I would open the door to let her in, but she wasn't there. Every night I would check the porch before I went to bed, but she wasn't there. I even left a fresh bowl of milk out for her every day, but it was never touched.

Then one morning, I opened the door, and there she was. She brushed her soft, fluffy black fur against my leg and purred her soft, sweet "I love you, Jill." "I love you, too, Blacky," I said. "I'm so glad you came home!"

Visual Images
Worksheet #1

Answer each of these questions about your paragraph.

1. Where could I have used more adjectives?

_____

2. Where could I have used more adverbs?

_____

3. What weak verbs could I replace with stronger verbs?

_____

4. What details could I add to make my paragraph more interesting?

_____

_____

5. What similes could I use to paint vivid word pictures?

_____

6. How can I do a better job of describing?

_____

7. Is there anything that needs to be taken out of my paragraph?

_____

_____

Visual Images

Worksheet #2

1. Read your paper and look for sentences that do not have end marks. Put end marks inside of circles at the end of each of those sentences.

2. Read your paper and look for sentences that do not begin with capital letters. **Underline three times** the letters that need to be capitalized.

3. Read your paper and look for proper nouns that do not begin with capital letters. **Underline three times** the letters that need to be capitalized.

4. Read your paper and look for words that are misspelled. Put a **circle** around each misspelled word.

When finished, trade papers with a partner and edit his or her paper.

Proofreading Marks

Add a letter or word.

Add a space.

Add a punctuation mark.

Take out something.

Make a capital letter.

Make a lowercase letter.

Word is spelled wrong.

Standards and Benchmarks: 3H, 4B

Using a Thesaurus

This activity helps your students add interest to their writing by substituting common words for more descriptive words.

Goal: The students will find and use synonyms of common words in writing.

Objectives

1. The student will use a thesaurus mini-book to find synonyms for common words.

2. The student will replace common words with more descriptive words in a story.

Materials

- copies of pages 87–91 for each student
- scissors
- stapler

Introduction

1. Explain to students that written work can be improved by substituting common words with interesting words.

2. Write the word *sad* on the chalkboard. Ask the students to think of synonyms for the word, such as *upset, unhappy, bummed, depressed, blue,* and *down.*

3. Explain to the students that synonyms for words can be found in a book called a *thesaurus.* Show them a thesaurus and look up common words, such as *happy, walk,* or *said,* sharing the synonyms listed in entries.

4. Explain to the students that the words in a thesaurus are listed in ABC order just like they are in a dictionary.

Group Activity

1. Divide the class into pairs. Write a common word on the chalkboard. Have each pair brainstorm a list of synonyms for the word.

2. Continue in this manner using a variety of common words.

3. Explain to the students that stories and other written work can be made more descriptive and interesting by using fewer commonly used words.

Using a Thesaurus *(cont.)*

Reinforcing the Skill

1. To assemble a mini-thesaurus, give each student a copy of pages 87–90. Students cut apart the pages, stack them in order, and staple them together along the left edge.

2. Allow the students to look through their thesauri to become familiar with the words on the pages. Write the word *said* on the chalkboard. Ask the students what letter is at the beginning of the word. Then have the students find the word in their thesauri. After finding it, have them read the synonyms for it.

3. Provide each student with a copy of the lesson worksheet. The student is asked to replace underlined words with synonyms found in the thesaurus.

4. Written Application: Instruct students to write a story on a selected topic. Then, working in partners, they are to identify common words used in the story. Have the partners either use their mini-thesauri to find synonyms for common words or brainstorm some of their own.

Computer Connection

Allow the students to type their stories using a word processing program. Show them how to use the thesaurus feature to find synonyms for common words.

Publishing Project

Display the students' revised and recopied stories on a bulletin board display, entitled "Interesting Words."

Evaluation

1. Lesson Objectives: Measure progress by reviewing each student's ability to find and use words in the thesaurus.

2. Written Application: Check each student's ability to use synonyms for common words by reading his or her written work. Use your choice of rubrics from pages 135–137. Based on the rubric score, determine the need for reteaching or further practice. Record skills mastery on the checklist on pages 138 and 139. If desired, have each student evaluate his or her own work using the self-assessment sheet on page 140.

Using a **Thesaurus** *(cont.)*

run
—flee
—jog
—rush
—scramble

Mini-Thesaurus

Name: _____

animal
beast
creature
critter

Page 1

eat
chew
chow
consume
dine
gobble
nibble
swallow

friend
buddy
chum
companion
pal
playmate

Page 2

good
great
marvelous
outstanding
sensational
splendid
super
wonderful

Page 3

Using a Thesaurus *(cont.)*

ground
earth
dirt
land
soil

happy
cheerful
ecstatic
elated
excited
glad
joyful

Page 4

house
abode
building
cabin
dwelling
home
lodge
residence
shelter

Page 5

laugh
chortle
chuckle
giggle
snicker

man
chap
fellow
gent
gentleman
guy
male

Page 6

pretty
attractive
beautiful
charming
good-looking
handsome
lovely

Page 7

Using a Thesaurus *(cont.)*

run

flee

jog

rush

scramble

scurry

speed

sprint

Page 8

sad

blue

bummed

depressed

disappointed

down

gloomy

sorrowful

uneasy

unhappy

upset

Page 9

said

answered

bellowed

declared

exclaimed

mentioned

replied

spoke

stated

uttered

voiced

whispered

yelled

Page 10

saw

discovered

examined

eyed

looked

noticed

observed

recognized

viewed

watched

witnessed

Page 11

Using a Thesaurus *(cont.)*

smile

beam

grin

smirk

student

kid

tot

youngster

youth

Page 12

walk

amble

march

pace

roam

shuffle

skip

step

stroll

wander

Page 13

went

cruised

departed

journeyed

left

took off

traveled

woman

dame

lady

female

Page 14

work

labor

strain

toil

Using a Thesaurus Worksheet

Write a synonym above each underlined word. Copy the new story on the lines below.

One day a <u>man</u> and his <u>child</u> left their <u>house</u>. They <u>walked</u> to the park. They wanted to play. They <u>ran</u> through the grass and <u>laughed</u>. The <u>man</u> and the <u>child</u> <u>saw</u> birds in the trees. They <u>saw</u> a <u>pretty</u> butterfly float by. It was a <u>great</u> day.

On the way home, the child saw his <u>friend</u>. He <u>said</u>, "Hi, David!"

They both <u>smiled</u>.

_____

_____

_____

_____

_____

_____

_____

_____

Standards and Benchmarks: 1H

Similes and Metaphors

Goal: The students will create similes and metaphors.

Objectives

1. The student will recognize similes.

2. The student will change similes into metaphors.

Materials

- chart paper
- markers
- copies of lesson worksheets (pages 94 and 95) for each student

Introduction

1. Explain to your students that *similes* and *metaphors* are more tools that can be used in writing to describe things creatively.

2. Similes and metaphors compare things. Show the examples below:

   Simile: The candy was as hard as a rock.

   Metaphor: The candy was a rock.

Explain that the simile and metaphor each compare the candy to a rock.

Group Activity—Simile

Write the following simile frame on chart paper:

_____ is as _____ as _____

Write snow in the first blank and ask the class to suggest descriptive words to fill in the other blanks. Follow the same procedure for *tree, honey,* and *puppy.*

Reinforcing the Skill

Provide each student with a copy of lesson worksheet #1 for additional practice.

Similes and Metaphors *(cont.)*

Group Activity—Metaphors

1. Explain to your students that metaphors are much like similes. Write the similes below on chart paper.

   The puppy was as soft as a pillow.

   The sandwich was as hard as a rock.

   The sky was as blue as a blueberry.

   The star was as sparkly as a diamond.

2. Explain that a metaphor can be made by removing words in the middle of each simile.

   The puppy was a pillow.

   The sandwich was a rock.

   The sky was a blueberry.

   The star was a diamond.

3. Write a list of similes on chart paper and instruct the students to suggest ways to change them into metaphors.

Reinforcing the Skill

1. Provide each student with lesson worksheet #2 for further practice of the skill.

2. Written Application: Encourage each student to write a paragraph or a story using at least one simile or metaphor.

Computer Connection

Display a document on your classroom computer containing incomplete similes or metaphors. Show students how to place the cursor at the end of each simile or metaphor and then type a word to complete it.

Evaluation

1. Lesson Objectives: Measure progress by reviewing each student's participation in the group activities and ability to complete the lesson worksheets.

2. Written Application: Review each student's written work for use of similes and/or metaphors. Use your choice of rubrics from pages 135–137 to evaluate each student's written work. Based on the rubric score, determine the need for reteaching or further practice. Record skills mastery on the checklist on pages 138 and 139. If desired, have each student evaluate his or her own work using the self-assessment sheet on page 140.

Similes and Metaphors

Worksheet #1

Write a simile for each object.

1. A teddy bear is

   as _____ as _____

2. The moon is

   as _____ as _____

3. Music is

   as _____ as _____

4. A bus is

   as _____ as _____

5. The sun is

   as _____ as _____

6. A night sky is

   as _____ as _____

7. A baby is

   as _____ as _____

8. A ladybug is

   as _____ as _____

Similes and Metaphors
Worksheet #2

Change each simile below into a metaphor. Recopy the sentence on the line.

1. The wind was as chilly as an ice cube.

   _____

2. Her cheeks were as red as apples.

   _____

3. The man was as tall as a tree.

   _____

4. The oven was as hot as a campfire.

   _____

5. The needle was as sharp as a knife.

   _____

6. My dad is as funny as a clown.

   _____

7. The sweater was as soft as a blanket.

   _____

8. The clouds were as fluffy as cotton.

   _____

9. The car was as loud as a train.

   _____

10. The kite was as high as an airplane.

   _____

Standards and Benchmarks: 1A, 1F, 1H

Similes in Poetry

Using similes in poetry and other writing is a good descriptive tool. A simile compares two very different things in a way that accentuates an attribute of each and helps to create a vivid word picture.

Goal: The students will use similes to write a descriptive list poem.

Objectives

1. The student will participate in a group writing of a list poem using similes.

2. The student will determine objects that could be described by familiar similes.

3. The student will write a list poem using similes.

Materials

- chart paper
- markers
- pictures from magazines or discarded calendars
- writing paper (with space for a picture)
- copies of pages 99 and 100 for each student

Introduction

1. Review with the students that similes compare attributes of two different things using *like* or *as* to paint a vivid word picture.

2. Assist the students in thinking of some of the similes of which they are familiar, such as:

   as light as a feather   *as dark as night*

   as cold as ice   *as hungry as a bear*

   as hard as a rock

3. Tell the students that using similes in poetry and writing is a helpful tool to make writing more descriptive.

Similes in Poetry *(cont.)*

Group Activity

1. Color a copy of the clown on page 99 and display it for the students. Ask them to tell you the features of the clown that stand out to them.

2. List on chart paper the features the students suggest, such as *hair, eyes, nose, mouth, hat, ears, feet,* and *clothes*.

   Now ask the students what it is about those features that made them noticeable. Record the suggestions beside each feature.

   > *hair—color*
   > *eyes—color and size*
   > *nose—color, size, and shape*
   > *ears—size*
   > *mouth—size*
   > *feet—size and shape*
   > *clothes–color and style*

3. Now ask the students to compare each of the attributes to another object with the same attribute. Record the answers on the chart paper.

   > *The hair is as orange as a pumpkin.*
   > *The eyes sparkle like diamonds.*
   > *The nose is as round as a button, or as big as an apple, or as red as cherries.*

4. Show the students how to change the information they have just gathered into a list poem. Start with a general statement of what is being described. List each attribute with a simile. Finish with another general statement of what is being described. For example:

   > *My funny clown has*
   > *Hair as orange as a pumpkin,*
   > *Eyes that sparkle like diamonds,*
   > *A nose as red as cherries,*
   > *A mouth as big as a hippo,*
   > *Ears that flop like an elephant's*
   > *And feet as flat as a duck's*
   > *That's my funny clown.*

Extension Activity

1. Give each student a copy of the clown picture to color.

2. Next, each student is to write similes to compare the attributes of the clown to other objects, and write a list poem to go with it.

3. Have the students share their poems with partners. The partners listen to determine whether the similes in the poems create vivid word pictures in their minds.

Similes in Poetry *(cont.)*

Reinforcing the Skill

1. Introduce the lesson worksheet on which the students are asked to write some objects that could be described by some familiar similes.

2. Show the students a variety of calendar or magazine pictures. Allow each student to choose a picture that appeals to him or her.

3. Have each student write a list of the object's attributes to describe with similes. Then have them write a simile comparing each attribute to another object.

4. Written Application: Have each student create a list poem as described in the Group Activity (page 97). Create student booklets by stapling together several sheets of writing paper. The first page will be the statement and a picture of what is being described. Each page after that will have one of the similes at the bottom and a drawing showing the featured attribute. The last page will be a drawing of the object and a general statement about it.

Publishing Project

Display the students' completed booklets for all to enjoy.

Evaluation

1. Lesson Objectives: Measure each student's progress by reviewing the performance on the lesson worksheet and the simile list poem.

2. Written Application: Use a selected rubric from pages 135-137 to evaluate progress. Record mastery on the skills checklist on pages 138 and 139. If desired, have each student use the self-assessment sheet on page 140 to evaluate his or her work.

Clown Pattern

Similes in Poetry Worksheet

For each simile, write two or more objects that could be described by it.

1. as hard as a rock

   _____

2. as lovely as a rose

   _____

3. as sweet as honey

   _____

4. as quiet as a mouse

   _____

5. as smooth as glass

   _____

6. as cuddly as a baby

   _____

7. as quick as a wink

   _____

8. as stubborn as a mule

   _____

Descriptive Writing

Color Description

Goal: The students will make artistic booklets about color.

Objectives

1. The student will participate in a class discussion.
2. The student will write descriptive sentences about color.

Materials

- copy of *Hailstones and Halibut Bones* by Mary O'Neill
- five sheets of chart paper
- marker
- copy of lesson worksheet (page 103) for each student
- construction paper
- stapler
- tempera paint
- paintbrush
- supply of magazine pictures

Introduction and Group Activity

1. Read *Hailstones and Halibut Bones*, drawing attention to the description of each color.
2. Post the chart paper along the walls. Label with the headings *looks, feels, sounds, smells, tastes.*
3. Select the color red and ask the students to think of things that "look" red. Encourage creativity when thinking of things that "taste" or "sound" red. For example, *red could taste like a fat, juicy strawberry.*

Red

looks	**feels**	**smells**
apples	hot	sweet
strawberries	fresh	spicy
jelly	smooth	
bubble gum		
fire truck		

	tastes	**sounds**
	juicy	loud
	tart	like a siren

Color Description *(cont.)*

Group Activity *(cont.)*

4. Show the students how the brainstormed lists can be used to write descriptions about the color red.

   Red is apples. Red feels smooth. Red smells spicy like pizza. Red tastes like a juicy strawberry. Red sounds like a siren.

Reinforcing the Skill

1. Distribute copies of lesson worksheet (page 103). The student completes the page by writing lists of words that describe each color.

2. Written Application: Have each student write a color description using the technique in the Group Activity (page 101).

3. For each sentence of the color description, have a student paint a picture. For example, "Red is apples," might have a picture of a tree filled with apples. Have the student write the accompanying sentence on each page.

4. After the paintings have dried, stack them together with a cover page and staple them together along the left edge.

Learning Center Activity

1. Place the magazine pictures at a learning center.

2. Encourage students to visit the center, select a picture, and think of ways to describe the colors.

Publishing Project

Display completed color booklets and invite students, administrators, and parents to enjoy them.

Evaluation

1. Lesson Objectives: Measure progress by reviewing each student's participation in the group activity and the learning center.

2. Written Application: Use your choice of rubrics from pages 135–137 to evaluate each student's written work. Record skills mastery on the checklist on pages 138 and 139. If desired, have each student evaluate his or her own work using the self-assessment sheet on page 140.

Color Description Worksheet

Write a list of words to describe each color.

Red
- looks _____   _____
- feels _____   _____
- tastes _____   _____
- smells _____   _____
- sounds _____   _____

Blue
- looks _____   _____
- feels _____   _____
- tastes _____   _____
- smells _____   _____
- sounds _____   _____

Green
- looks _____   _____
- feels _____   _____
- tastes _____   _____
- smells _____   _____
- sounds _____   _____

Purple
- looks _____   _____
- feels _____   _____
- tastes _____   _____
- smells _____   _____
- sounds _____   _____

Yellow
- looks _____   _____
- feels _____   _____
- tastes _____   _____
- smells _____   _____
- sounds _____   _____

Choose a color:
- looks _____   _____
- feels _____   _____
- tastes _____   _____
- smells _____   _____
- sounds _____   _____

Standards and Benchmarks: 1A, 1F, 1H

Rhyming

Goal: The students will create pairs of rhyming words.

Objectives

1. The student will sing rhyming songs.

2. The student will identify pairs of rhyming words.

Materials

- copy of a poetry book
- chart paper
- marker
- copy of page 106
- copy of lesson worksheet (page 107) for each student

Introduction

1. Begin the lesson by singing a familiar rhyming song, such as "I Know an Old Lady Who Swallowed a Fly." Omit the final rhyming word in each verse and allow the students to provide it.

   I know an old lady who swallowed a fly.

   I don't know why she swallowed a fly.

   I guess she'll _____.

2. Try this technique with other rhyming songs. This will show your students how natural it is to make rhymes.

   Suggested rhyming songs:

   "I've Been Working on the Railroad"

   "I'm a Little Teapot"

   "Twinkle, Twinkle, Little Star"

   "A-Hunting We Will Go"

   "The Itsy Bitsy Spider"

   Example:

   The itsy bitsy spider went up the water spout.

   Down came the rain and washed the spider _____.

   Out came the sun and dried up all the rain.

   And the itsy bitsy spider went up the spout _____.

Rhyming *(cont.)*

Group Activity

1. Read rhyming poetry to your students. As you read, have them identify the words that rhyme. Write the words on the chalkboard.

2. Write several one- or two-syllable words on chart paper and ask the students to think of words that rhyme with each.

Learning Center Activity

Duplicate the picture cards on page 106. Cut them apart and place them at a learning center. To participate, a student matches the rhyming pictures.

Reinforcing the Skill

1. Provide each student with a copy of the lesson worksheet.

2. Have the students work with partners to find rhyming words in poetry books.

3. Written Application: Encourage the students to make lists of rhyming words. Store these lists in a writing notebook for later use in poetry writing.

Publishing Project

On a bulletin board display, have the students post drawings of rhyming words, such as *hat* and *cat* or *ride* and *slide*.

Computer Connection

1. Using a desktop publishing program, allow the students to find pictures of words that rhyme.

2. Print the graphics and have the students label the pictures.

Evaluation

1. Lesson Objectives: Measure each student's progress by reviewing the participation in the group activity and ability to identify and create pairs of rhyming words.

2. Written Application: Record mastery on the skills checklist on pages 138 and 139.

Rhyming *(cont.)*

Rhyming Picture Cards

Rhyming Worksheet

Write three or four words that rhyme with each word below.

hat

_____
_____
_____
_____

frog

_____
_____
_____
_____

day

_____
_____
_____
_____

cake

_____
_____
_____
_____

sky

_____
_____
_____
_____

sun

_____
_____
_____
_____

Standards and Benchmarks: 1A, 1F, 1H

Writing Couplets

Goal: The students will use rhyming words to create couplets.

Objectives

1. The student will identify rhyming word pairs.

2. The student will use rhyming words to create couplets

Materials

- poetry book
- chart paper
- marker
- copy of lesson worksheet (page 109) for each student

Introduction

Review rhyming words with your students by singing a rhyming song or by reading from a students' poetry book. Encourage the students to name the rhyming words they hear.

Group Activity

1. Write the following couplet on chart paper:

   A little, tiny mouse,

   is creeping through the house.

2. Have the students identify the two rhyming words—mouse and house. Call attention to the use of the rhyming words at the end of each phrase.

3. Write the words *cat* and *mat* on the chalkboard. Invite the students to think of rhyming phrases using these words.

Reinforcing the Skill

1. Provide each student with a copy of the lesson worksheet to complete.

2. Written Application: Encourage each student to write his or her own couplets using the list of rhyming words from the previous lesson on rhymes.

Evaluation

1. Lesson Objectives: Measure each student's progress by reviewing the participation in the group activity and ability to complete the lesson worksheet.

2. Written Application: Use your choice of rubrics from pages 135–137 to evaluate each student's written work. Based on the rubric score, determine the need for reteaching or further practice. Record skills mastery on the checklist on pages 138 and 139. If desired, have each student evaluate his or her own work using the self-assessment sheet on page 140.

Couplets

Complete each couplet with a rhyming word.

Let's go out and play, it's a lovely _____.	
I saw a snake swimming in a _____.	
There is a mouse in my _____.	
My little white cat sat on a _____.	
One, two, three, what do you _____.	
Mom will bake the chocolate _____.	
In our car we traveled _____.	

Standards and Benchmarks: 1A, 1H

Writing Cinquain Poetry

Poetry writing is a great way to put descriptive writing skills to use.

Goal: The students will use descriptive words to write cinquain poetry.

Objectives

1. The student will participate in a group writing of poetry.

2. The student will brainstorm descriptive words for use in poems.

3. The student will write cinquain poems.

Materials

- copy of a children's poetry book, such as *Random House Book of Poetry for Children* (See the bibliography on page 141.)
- chart paper and marker
- two copies of page 112 for each student
- copy of page 113 for each student
- writing paper

Introduction

1. Read several poems, then discuss the use of adjectives, adverbs, similes, metaphors, and other descriptive language.

Group Activity

1. Select a topic for a poem, such as *rain*. Hang four sheets of chart paper on the walls. Label each with a different heading—*adjectives, verbs, sentences, renaming nouns*.

2. Brainstorm words or phrases about rain for each of the headings. Write responses on the chart paper. For example:

Adjectives	**Verbs**
wet	falling
cold	splashing
damp	pouring

Sentences	**Renaming Nouns**
It makes me feel cozy.	pitter patter
It falls from the clouds.	storm
I love to splash in the puddles.	

Writing Cinquain Poetry *(cont.)*

Group Activity *(cont.)*

3. Draw the cinquain template (page 112) on another sheet of chart paper. Insert words and phrases from the brainstormed lists to complete the poem.

Rain

Wet, damp

falling, splashing, pouring

It falls from the clouds

Pitter patter

Reinforcing the Skill

1. Distribute copies of page 112 and have students write new poems about rain. They may use words from the lists or select words of their own.

2. Written Application: Provide each student with a copy of page 113 and a clean copy of page 112. Have the student select a topic, brainstorm words for each of the categories, and write a poem on the template.

Publishing Project

Encourage the students to recopy their poems on writing paper and create illustrations to display with their work.

Computer Connection

Have the students use a word processing program to type their poems. Demonstrate how to add computer graphics from the program's library of graphics or from another source.

Evaluation

1. Lesson Objectives: Measure each student's progress by reviewing the participation in the group activity and ability to complete a cinquain poem.

2. Written Application: Use your choice of rubrics from pages 135–137 to evaluate each student's written work. Record skills mastery on the checklist on pages 138 and 139. If desired, have each student evaluate his or her own work using the self-assessment sheet on page 140.

Cinquain Template

_____
topic

_____, _____,
adjective,   adjective

_____, _____, _____,
verb,   verb,   verb

_____
sentence

_____
renaming noun

Copy your poem onto another sheet of paper and make an illustration to go with it.

Cinquain Brainstorming Sheet

Topic: _____

Nouns

_____   _____

_____   _____

_____   _____

Verbs

_____   _____

_____   _____

_____   _____

Sentences

_____

_____

_____

_____

Renaming Nouns

_____   _____

_____   _____

Standards and Benchmarks: 1A, 1B, 1H

Onomatopoeia

Goal: The students will use onomatopoeia in writing.

Objectives

1. The student will identify the sounds made by animals and objects.

2. The student will use onomatopoeia in writing.

Materials

- copy of page 116, cut into onomatopoeia word cards
- copy of lesson worksheet (page 117) for each student
- paper bag
- writing paper

Introduction

1. Discuss with your students that many things make sounds. These sounds can be used in writing to add interest.

2. Ask your students to think of the sounds made by different animals and objects.

Group Activity

1. To prepare for this activity, write the following passage on chart paper, including the underlines:

   One day I went for a walk. The <u>birds</u> were singing. The <u>wind</u> was blowing through the trees. Across the street, I heard a barking <u>dog</u>. It was playing with a young girl. She was laughing as she played. Soon, it began to rain. I could see the <u>raindrops</u> falling on the sidewalk. I pretended to be a <u>hopping</u> <u>bunny</u> all the way back to my house.

2. Begin the activity by discussing sounds made by other things. List students' ideas on chart paper. Explain that words that represent sounds are examples of onomatopoeia.

3. Read the prepared passage to the class, emphasizing the underlined words.

4. Ask the students to think of sounds that could be made by the underlined words. Then rewrite the story and read it together.

5. Discuss the difference between the two stories, pointing out how the onomatopoeias in the second story generated interest.

Onomatopoeia *(cont.)*

Learning Center Activity

1. Place the onomatopoeia cards in a paper bag at a learning center along with a supply of writing paper.

2. To participate in the learning center, a student begins to write a story. He or she then randomly selects an onomatopoeia word card from the bag. The student continues writing the story, adding the sound to it in some way.

3. The student continues to select cards from the bag and add onomatopoeia to the story.

Reinforcing the Skill

1. Distribute copies of the lesson worksheet to the students. Each student writes a sound word for each of the words on the page.

2. Written Application: Instruct each student to write a story, including onomatopoeia where appropriate.

Publishing Project

Have each student type his or her story using a word processing program. Show the students how to italicize each onomatopoeia.

Evaluation

1. Lesson Objectives: Measure progress by reviewing each student's participation in the group activity and ability to complete the lesson worksheet.

2. Written Application: Check each student's ability to use onomatopoeia in writing. Use your choice of rubrics from pages 135–137 to evaluate each student's written work. Based on the rubric score, determine the need for reteaching or further practice. Record skills mastery on the checklist on pages 138 and 139. If desired, have each student evaluate his or her own work using the self-assessment sheet on page 140.

Onomatopoeia Word Cards

chirp	drip, drip
woosh	shh
pitter patter	beep
squeak	honk
moo	yee haa!
varoom	boing
ding dong	woof
plink, plink	splat
crash	la, la, la

Onomatopoeia Worksheet

Write a sound word for each word below.

1. horn _____

2. train _____

3. hopping _____

4. rain _____

5. thunder _____

6. door slam _____

7. a punch _____

8. cat _____

9. music _____

10. wind _____

11. mouse _____

12. lion _____

13. cooking bacon _____

14. lawn mower _____

Standards and Benchmarks: 1H

Idioms

Goal: The students will use idioms to add description to writing.

Objectives

1. The student will identify idioms.

2. The student will determine the meaning of idioms.

3. The student will use idioms in writing.

Materials

- copy of *The King Who Rained* by Fred Gwynne or *Amelia Bedelia* by Peggy Parish, or any other book of idioms (See the bibliography on page 141.)
- chart paper
- marker
- copy of lesson worksheet (page 121) for each student
- copy of pages 122–123, cut into cards

Common Idioms

a fork in the road

a frog in my throat

take a load off your feet

stopped dead in her tracks

a broken heart

bite off more than you can chew

swept off your feet

step on the gas

monkey around

you changed your mind

costs an arm and a leg

got up on the wrong side of the bed

keep an eye on

stay in touch

read my mind

zip your lip

Idioms *(cont.)*

Introduction

1. Explain to students that figurative language can be used to add interest to writing.

2. Read a book of idioms, such as *The King Who Rained* or *Amelia Bedelia* to the students.

3. Write a list of idioms (see page 118) on chart paper and discuss the literal and figurative meaning of each.

4. After discussing the meaning of each idiom, have some fun with this concept by having each student illustrate the literal meaning of an idiom. For example, "There was a fork in the road," could be illustrated by showing a dinner fork lying on a street.

Group Activity

As a class, use the list of idioms (on the chart paper) to write a paragraph. See the example below.

> *One day I woke up on the wrong side of the bed. I was feeling under the weather and it was raining cats and dogs outside. I had so much to do. I knew I had bit off more than I could chew. I told my mom she could count on me to do my chores. I knew I shouldn't complain, so I zipped my lips and stepped on the gas. When I finished my chores, I sat down to take a load off my feet. My mom said, "You deserve a nice treat for your hard work." She read my mind!*

Reinforcing the Skill

1. Provide the students with copies of the lesson worksheet on page 121. The students are asked to tell what each idiom means.

2. Allow the students to work with partners for assistance.

3. Written Application: Using the displayed chart-paper list, have each student write a paragraph using at least three idioms.

Idioms *(cont.)*

Learning Center Activity

1. Place the idiom cards in a learning center.

2. To participate in the center, a student chooses an idiom card and illustrates it with the literal or idiomatic definition.

Publishing Project

1. Combine students' literal illustrations of idioms in a class booklet.

2. Display the paragraphs from the Written Application on a bulletin board entitled "Figuratively Speaking."

Computer Connection

Encourage students to create computer-generated illustrations of idioms by using a graphics or drawing program.

Evaluation

1. Lesson Objectives: Measure progress by reviewing each student's participation in the group activity and the ability to complete the lesson worksheet and learning center.

2. Written Application: Review each student's paragraph for use of idioms. Use your choice of rubrics from pages 135–137 to evaluate each student's written work. Based on the rubric score, determine the need for reteaching or further practice. Record skills mastery on the checklist on pages 138 and 139. If desired, have each student evaluate his or her own work using the self-assessment sheet on page 140.

Idioms

Write the figurative meaning of each idiom below.

1. Take a load off your feet.

   _____

2. It broke my heart.

   _____

3. You're pulling my leg!

   _____

4. Keep an eye on your brother.

   _____

5. Zip your lips.

   _____

6. You can count on me.

   _____

7. It's raining cats and dogs.

   _____

8. I stopped dead in my tracks.

   _____

9. I could eat a horse.

   _____

10. I'm feeling under the weather.

    _____

    _____

11. Don't monkey around.

    _____

    _____

12. The toy costs an arm and a leg.

    _____

    _____

Idiom Cards

a frog in my throat

step on the gas

bit off more than he
could chew

under the weather

Idiom Cards *(cont.)*

got up on the wrong
side of the bed

zip your lip

a fork in the road

raining cats and dogs

Standards and Benchmarks: 1A, 1B, 1H

Alliteration

Goal: The students will use alliteration in written work.

Objectives

1. The student will brainstorm words beginning with the same letter.

2. The student will create sentences using many words with the same beginning letter.

3. The student will use alliteration in written work.

Materials

- chart paper
- marker
- 10 index cards
- a paper lunch bag
- copies of lesson worksheets (pages 126 and 127) for each student

Introduction

1. Review with your students the many ways to add interest to writing using descriptive tools.

2. Explain that *alliteration* is another tool that can be used. Define alliteration as *the use of words that begin with the same letter.*

Group Activity

1. Write the letter *s* on chart paper. Ask the students to think of words (nouns, verbs, adjectives, adverbs, etc.) that begin with the letter *s*.

2. Show the students how the words can be used to make alliterative sentences, such as:

   The silly snake slithered slowly on the sparkling sand.
   Some sensational salamanders sang sweetly in September.

3. Experiment with alliteration in the same manner using several different beginning letters.

Learning Center Activity

1. Write different letters of the alphabet on index cards and place them in a paper bag at a learning center. (Use letters such as *b, c, d, l, m, n, p, r, s,* and *t.*)

2. A student randomly selects a letter card and makes a list of words beginning with that letter. The student then writes several sentences using words from his or her list.

Alliteration *(cont.)*

Reinforcing the Skill

1. Provide each student with a copy of lesson worksheet #1 on page 126. The student completes the page by writing lists of words beginning with the same letter.

2. For an added challenge, provide each student with a copy of worksheet #2 (page 127). The student reads a series of sentences and then uses words in the word bank to replace underlined words to create alliterative sentences.

3. Written Application: Instruct each student to select a topic of interest. The student brainstorms a list of words beginning with the same letter as the topic. Then the student writes a story or paragraph, incorporating alliteration into the writing.

Publishing Project

1. Have each student create an illustration of alliterative sentences to post on a bulletin board display.

2. Encourage the students to read classmates' sentences and respond to the use of alliteration.

Computer Connection

Help your students find new words beginning with a particular beginning letter by showing them how to use the thesaurus feature of a word processing program. For example, if a student wants to find a synonym for walk that begins with the letter *s*, the student types the word, highlights it, and then selects the thesaurus. A list of synonyms will appear. The student looks for a word beginning with *s* and then selects it to replace the typed word on the document.

Evaluation

1. Lesson Objectives: Measure progress by reviewing each student's participation in the group activity, learning center, and ability to complete the lesson worksheets.

2. Written Application: Review each student's alliterative sentences and story or paragraph about a selected topic, checking for use of alliteration. Use your choice of rubrics from pages 135–137 to evaluate each student's written work. Based on the rubric score, determine the need for reteaching or further practice. Record skills mastery on the checklist on pages 138 and 139. If desired, have each student evaluate his or her own work using the self-assessment sheet on page 140.

Alliteration

Worksheet #1

Write a list of words beginning with each letter below.

T

_____

_____

_____

_____

H

_____

_____

_____

_____

W

_____

_____

_____

_____

R

_____

_____

_____

_____

C

_____

_____

_____

_____

F

_____

_____

_____

_____

On the back of this paper, write sentences using many of the words in each list.

126

Alliteration

Worksheet #2

Create alliterative sentences. Replace each underlined word with a word from the word bank. Recopy each sentence on the line below it.

c words

1. The cat <u>sat</u> on the <u>pillow</u> and meowed.

_____

s words

2. One Saturday a <u>funny</u> <u>reptile</u> <u>moved</u> in the dirt.

_____

t words

3. <u>Five</u> <u>little</u> turtles <u>walked</u> to the <u>city</u>.

_____

w words

4. The <u>cold</u> <u>breeze</u> <u>blew</u> past the <u>lake</u>.

_____

p words

5. The <u>rain</u> <u>sprinkled</u> down on the <u>street</u>.

_____

b words

6. The <u>animal</u> ate <u>food</u> for <u>a meal</u>.

_____

Word Bank			
wind	winter	tiny	slithered
silly	poured	snake	sand
pitter patter	cushion	breakfast	cried
berries	trotted	curled up	
water	bear	pavement	
town	two	whipped	

Descriptive Writing Review

Goal: The students will demonstrate knowledge of various descriptive writing tools.

Objectives

1. The student will identify different types of descriptive language.

2. The student will use different types of descriptive language.

Materials

- gameboard (pages 129 and 130)
- game cards (page 131)
- game die
- copies of page 132

Introduction

1. Review with your students the different kinds of descriptive writing tools, including adjectives, adverbs, visual images, similes, metaphors, and idioms.

2. Encourage the students to provide examples for each.

Review Game

1. Duplicate the gameboard and cards on pages 129–131. Cut the cards apart.

2. Color and laminate the gameboard and cards, if desired. Make the game self-checking by duplicating and cutting out the answer key on page 144. Use coins or other small objects for game pieces.

3. To play, a student selects a card, determines the type of descriptive tool, and checks his or her answer on the answer key.

Testing

1. Provide each student with a copy of the descriptive writing test on page 132. Ask the student to identify and use different kinds of descriptive writing. Use the results of the test to help determine the need for further practice of the skills.

Directions for two players:

1. Place the cards facedown.

2. Place the game pieces on START.

3. A player selects a card and names the descriptive writing tool.

4. Check the answer key. If correct, roll the die and move. If incorrect, do not move. Next player selects a card.

5. The first player to reach FINISH is the winner.

Descriptive Writing Game

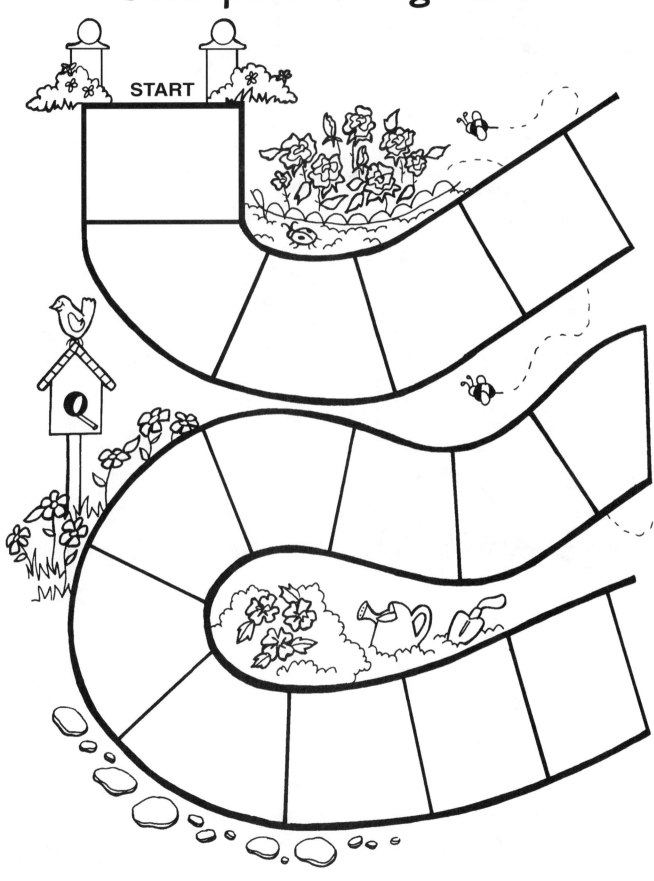

START

Descriptive Writing Game *(cont.)*

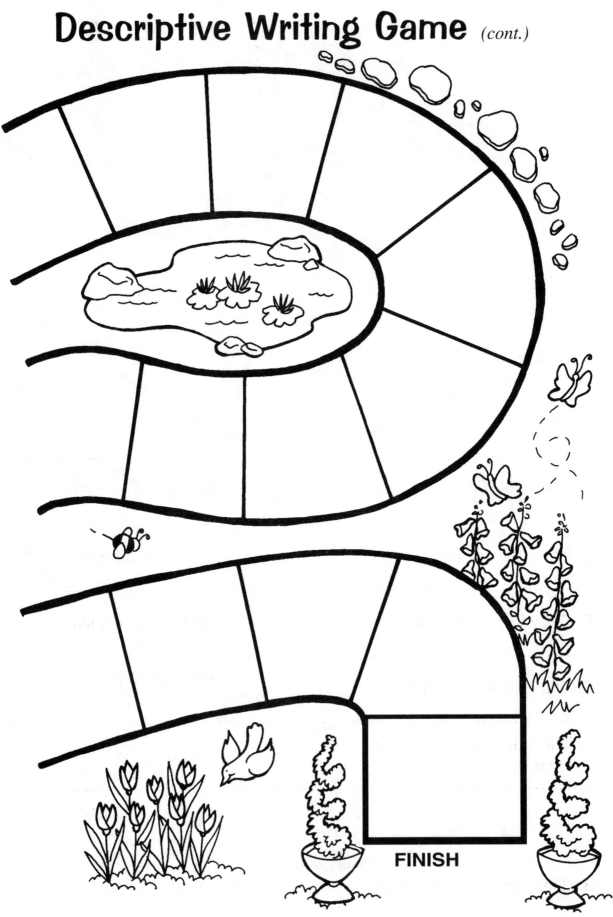

FINISH

Descriptive Writing Game Cards

1. The boy played happily.	14. Don't beat around the bush.
2. They screamed loudly.	15. She was as happy as a clam.
3. Her hair was curly and brown.	16. The snake hissed, "Sssssssss."
4. The train went clickety clack down the track.	17. He rested peacefully.
5. She saw a tall, green tree.	18. Her eyes were as blue as the sky.
6. The lake was a mirror.	19. His hair is as brown as chocolate.
7. We came to a fork in the road.	20. I am as warm as toast.
8. They ate quickly.	21. The tree was a tower.
9. Did you change your mind?	22. Her scream was a siren.
10. The rain was a song.	Move two spaces and take another turn.
11. The warm cookies tasted sweet.	Lose your turn.
12. I have a broken heart.	Move three spaces and take another turn.
13. "Hee hee," she laughed.	Go back one space.

Descriptive Writing Test

1. Write three adjectives to describe **rain**. _____

2. Is this a simile or a metaphor?

   The frog was as green as grass. _____

3. Write two synonyms for the word *cold*. _____

4. Which one of the sentences below contains an idiom? Circle it.

   It's raining cats and dogs.

   The two boys slowly walked on the dusty road.

5. Write onomatopoeia for each object below.

   bell _____

   train _____

   dog _____

   ocean _____

6. Finish the couplet below.

   We are having fun.

   Playing in the _____.

7. Write three adverbs for the word *walks*.

   He walks _____.

   He walks _____.

   He walks _____.

Using Rubrics

Why Use a Rubric?

Using rubrics to assess student work helps you and your students identify quality work. Using rubrics to grade your students' work will save time and make the task easier. Each step of the four-point rubric describes the requirements needed in order to receive that score. This will help you convey to students and parents the areas of strengths and weaknesses in written assignments.

What is a Four-point Rubric?

A four-point rubric is a scale that represents different levels of writing. Each level outlines skills demonstrated in writing. You can find several rubrics on pages 135–137.

A *four-point response* indicates that the student incorporates all the requirements for the assignment. A four-point score indicates that very little improvement is needed.

A *three-point score* indicates that the student incorporates most of the requirements for the assignment. There may be a few errors, but the writing or project is clear and has only a slight need for improvement.

A *two-point response* indicates that the student exhibits many errors in the content of the assignment. The writing or project tends to be unclear and illogically sequenced. Significant revision is needed to improve the work.

A *one-point response* indicates weak writing skills or quality of the project with the need for improvement in a variety of areas. This score often demonstrates the need for reteaching and careful revision.

How Do I Create My Own Rubric?

This book provides several rubrics to use for assessing your students' work. These include mechanics, content and organization, basic visual aids, maps and diagrams, and charts and graphs. However, you may find it is necessary to create your own rubric to meet the needs of your students and the specific lessons you teach. Use the following steps to create your own rubric:

1. Determine the goal of the assignment.

2. Select criteria for the highest performance of the assignment.

3. Determine whether you would like to create a three- or four-point rubric.

4. Write the criteria for the descending levels. Keep in mind that the one-point score usually involves the absence of most of the requirements of the assignment.

Using Rubrics *(cont.)*

Use this frame to help create your rubric:

Scoring Rubric

4 points:

-
-
-

3 points:

-
-
-

2 points:

-
-
-

1 point:

-
-
-

Using Rubrics *(cont.)*

Writing Mechanics

4 points:

The student consistently spells high-frequency words correctly. Proper end marks and commas in a series are used. The student consistently capitalizes the first word of a sentence. The student capitalizes proper nouns. Sentences are complete and use proper noun/verb agreement.

3 points:

The student's writing is relatively free of spelling errors. Most of the sentences contain proper end marks and commas. Capital letters are used at the beginning of most sentences and proper nouns. The writing is grammatically correct and sentences are complete.

2 points:

The writing includes some spelling errors. The writing has inconsistent use of end marks and capitalization. The writing has some evidence of incomplete sentences.

1 point:

The writing contains many spelling, punctuation, and capitalization errors. Incorrect grammar and incomplete sentences dominate the work.

Using Rubrics *(cont.)*

Content and Organization

4 points:

The piece is clearly written and contains a central purpose. The work contains descriptive words and details to make the writing interesting. All information is relevant to the purpose of the piece. Sentences are complete and written in logical sequence.

3 points:

The piece is clearly written and contains a fairly clear purpose. The work contains some descriptive words and details to make the writing interesting. Most of the information is relevant to the purpose of the piece. Most of the sentences are complete and written in logical sequence.

2 points:

The writing's purpose is somewhat unclear. Few descriptive words and details are used to make the piece interesting. Some irrelevant information is included. The writing contains some incomplete sentences and logical sequence is not always used.

1 point:

The purpose of the writing is unclear. The piece does not contain descriptive words or details. Irrelevant information is included. Most sentences are not complete and/or do not follow a logical sequence.

Using Rubrics *(cont.)*

Descriptive Writing

4 points:

The piece is clearly written and contains a central purpose. The student utilizes descriptive language as shown by the use of adjectives, adverbs, similes, sensory writing, etc. The work includes details to make the writing interesting. The work contains complete sentences, is easy to understand, and paints visual images for the reader.

3 points:

The piece is clearly written and contains a fairly clear purpose. The student utilizes some descriptive language as shown by the use of adjectives, adverbs, similes, sensory writing, etc. The work includes some detail to make the writing interesting. The work may or may not contain complete sentences or paint visual images for the reader.

2 points:

The purpose of the piece is somewhat unclear. The student does not use many adjectives, adverbs, or other descriptive language. The work contains few details. The work may or may not contain complete sentences. The piece does not create a visual image for the reader.

1 point:

The piece is unclear. The student does not use descriptive language. The work lacks relevant details, contains numerous incomplete sentences, and does not paint a visual image for the reader.

Basic Skills Checklist

Name: _____

Prewriting

discusses ideas with peers. . . . . ❑

draws pictures to generate ideas . . . . ❑

Drafting and Revising

rereads . . . . ❑

rearranges words, sentences, paragraphs . . . . ❑

adds descriptive words and details. . . . . ❑

incorporates suggestions from others. . . . . ❑

Editing and Publishing

proofreads. . . . . ❑

edits grammar, punctuation, spelling, etc.. . . . . ❑

Evaluates own and others' writing

asks questions about writing . . . . ❑

makes comments about writing . . . . ❑

helps apply grammatical and mechanical conventions . . . . ❑

Uses logical sequence

includes beginning, middle, end. . . . . ❑

Uses detailed descriptions

describes people, places, and things . . . . ❑

Basic Skills Checklist *(cont.)*

Name: _____

Writes in a variety of formats

Grammatical and mechanical conventions

—uses complete sentences . . . . ❏

—uses declarative sentences . . . . ❏

—uses interrogative sentences . . . . ❏

—uses nouns . . . . ❏

—uses verbs . . . . ❏

—uses adjectives . . . . ❏

—uses adverbs . . . . ❏

—uses proper spelling . . . . ❏

—uses resources to spell correctly . . . . ❏

—capitalizes beginning of sentences . . . . ❏

—capitalizes proper nouns . . . . ❏

—uses proper end marks . . . . ❏

—uses commas in a series . . . . ❏

Gathers and uses information for research purposes

—generates questions about topics of interest . . . . ❏

—uses books to gather information for research topics . . . . ❏

Comments:

_____

_____

_____

_____

Writing Self-Assessment

Read your writing and make corrections. Use the checklist below to help you.

○ My writing is neat and easy to read.

○ I capitalized proper nouns.

○ I used correct end marks.

○ I indented my paragraphs.

○ I used correct spelling.

○ I used complete sentences.

○ I included adjectives to describe nouns.

○ I included adverbs to describe verbs.

○ I included similes and other visual images.

○ I included important details.

○ My writing paints a picture for the reader.

○ I had a classmate read my work.

Bibliography

Gwynne, Fred. *The King who Rained.* Aladdin, 1988.

Heller, Ruth. *Kites Sail High: A Book About Verbs.* Paper Star, 1998.

Heller, Ruth. *Many Luscious Lollipops: A Book About Adjectives.* Paper Star, 1998.

Heller, Ruth. *Merry Go Round: A Book About Nouns.* Paper Star, 1998.

Heller, Ruth. *Up, Up and Away: A Book About Adverbs.* Paper Star, 1998.

Leigh, Tom. *The Sesame Street Word Book.* Golden Books, 1998.

Mayer, Mercer. *Little Monster's Word Book.* Inchworm Press, 1998.

O'Neill, Mary. *Hailstones and Halibut Bones: Adventures in Color.* Doubleday, 1990.

Parish, Peggy. *Amelia Bedelia.* Harpercollins, 1992.

Prelutsky, Jack and Arnold Lobel (illustrators). *Random House Book of Poetry for Children.* Random House, 1983.

Shannon, David. *No, David.* Scholastic, 1998.

Shannon, David. *David Goes to School.* Blue Sky Press, 1999.

Wilder, Laura Ingalls. *On the Banks of Plum Creek.* HarperCollins Juvenile Books, 1953.

Answer Key

Page 11

The following words should be circled:

apple

ball

bat

boat

book

boy

desk

dish

dog

door

dress

flower

friend

hair

monkey

paper

pizza

school

tree

water

Page 21

1. nibbled
2. tiptoed
3. stomped
4. gobbled
5. glanced
6. stared
7. paced
8. gazed
9. devoured
10. strolled
11. roared
12. whispered
13. cried
14. sighed

Page 30

1. slowly
2. loudly
3. sadly
4. happily
5. angrily
6. softly
7. quickly
8. silently
9. fast
10. slowly
11. quietly
12. politely

Page 31

1. first, when
2. prettily, how
3. beautifully, how
4. finally, when
5. next, when
6. quietly, how
7. quickly, how
8. softly, how
9. swiftly, how
10. now, when
11. loudly, how
12. nicely, how
13. politely, how
14. then, when

Page 32

Accept reasonable alternatives. Possible responses:

1. Turn the music on softly.
2. Come and get me soon.
3. Walk past the sleeping lion quietly.
4. Say, "Good morning," cheerfully.
5. Eat politely.
6. Speak loudly.

Page 37

1. The triceratops has three horns.
2. My friend, Cristy, likes dinosaurs.
3. My sister and I like to read books about dinosaurs.
4. When we go to the museum, we will see the dinosaurs.
5. The triceratops is a dinosaur.
6. When Andrew found a bone, he thought it belonged to a dinosaur.
7. At Safeway, there was a book about dinosaurs.

Answer Key *(cont.)*

8. Yesterday, I saw a video about the triceratops.
9. My mom said that I know a lot about dinosaurs.
10. Dinosaurs are my favorite things.
11. At school we learned about triceratops.
12. When I dig in the sand, I hope I will find a dinosaur bone.

Page 38

Beginning: Digging for dinosaur bones is fun.

I: When I grow up, I want to hunt for dinosaurs.

Proper Noun: I think my friends, Kyle and Amy like dinosaurs, too.

Page 42

1. period/statement
2. question mark/question
3. exclamation mark/exclamation
4. exclamation mark/exclamation *or* command/period
5. period/command
6. question mark/question
7. question mark/question
8. period/statement
9. period/command
10. exclamation mark/exclamation
11. exclamation mark/exclamation
12. period/statement

Page 60

day
did
down
then
to
two
off
only
our
had
has
have
went
will
would
saw
see
some

Page 61

1. and, are, as
2. be, because, been
3. her, here, him
4. like, little, look
5. who, will, with
6. then, there, they
7. see, she, so
8. no, not, now
9. me, more, my
10. if, into, is
11. first, for, from
12. go, going, got
13. off, on, one
14. were, what, when

Page 62

<u>When</u> I was <u>little</u> I did not <u>like</u> to eat vegetables. My mom <u>would</u> try <u>very</u> hard to <u>make</u> me eat them. <u>She</u> <u>said</u> I needed to eat vegetables so I <u>could</u> grow strong. I didn't care. I still didn't want to eat <u>them</u>. Now I am older and I <u>have</u> learned to like some vegetables. <u>I</u> <u>will</u> eat salads and broccoli. <u>My</u> mom says <u>she</u> is proud of me. <u>When</u> I grow up, I'm <u>going</u> to be healthy and strong.

Page 69

Accept reasonable alternatives. Possible responses:
1. tree
2. kitten
3. apple pie
4. skateboard
5. eyes
6. bed
7. shoes
8. student
9. fire
10. sky

Answer Key *(cont.)*

Page 79

My sister is funny.
She wears the strangest clothes I have ever seen.
My sister even dyed her hair blue.

I love to watch my mother cook.
Everything she makes smells so good.
Sometimes she lets me lick the bowl.
She gives me little bites of my favorite foods.
I am learning to be a good cook by watching her.

Page 95

1. The wind was an ice cube.
2. Her cheeks were apples.
3. The man was a tree.
4. The oven was a campfire.
5. The needle was a knife.
6. My dad is a clown.
7. The sweater was a blanket.
8. The clouds were cotton.
9. The car was a train.
10. The kite was an airplane.

Page 121

Accept reasonable alternatives. Possible responses:

1. Sit down and relax.
2. I felt very sad.
3. You're teasing me!
4. Watch your brother.
5. Don't say anything.
6. You can depend on me.
7. It's raining very hard.
8. I stopped right away.
9. I'm very hungry.
10. I'm feeling sick.
11. Don't act silly.
12. The toy costs a lot of money.

Page 127

1. The cat curled up on the cushion and cried.
2. One Saturday a silly snake slithered in the sand.
3. Two tiny turtles trotted to town.
4. The winter wind whipped past the water.

5. The pitter-patter poured down on the pavement.
6. The bear ate berries for breakfast.

Page 131

1. adverb
2. adverb
3. adjectives
4. onomatopoeia
5. adjectives
6. metaphor
7. idiom
8. adverb
9. idiom
10. metaphor
11. adjectives
12. idiom
13. onomatopoeia
14. idiom
15. idiom or simile
16. onomatopoeia
17. adverb
18. simile
19. simile
20. simile
21. metaphor
22. metaphor

Page 132

1. Accept appropriate adjectives for rain.
2. simile
3. Accept appropriate synonyms for cold.
4. It's raining cats and dogs.
5. Accept reasonable answers.
6. Accept any appropriate word that rhymes with fun.
7. Accept reasonable adverbs such as quickly, slowly, happily, briskly, rapidly, sadly.